THE SECRET LOVES OF
Geek Girls

Edited by Hope Nicholson

Bedside
Press

The Secret Loves of Geek Girls © 2015

Introduction © 2015, Hope Nicholson
Foreword © 2015, Trina Robbins

Front cover art: Gisèle Lagacé & Shouri
"Secret Loves of Geek Girls" Logo: Rachel Deering
"Bedside Press" Logo: Genevieve FT
Back cover art: Jen Bartel
Book design: Megan Lavey-Heaton

Library and Archives Canada Cataloguing in Publication

The Secret Loves of Geek Girls / editor, Hope Nicholson.

ISBN 978-0-9939970-1-3 (paperback)
ISBN 978-0-9939970-2-0 (pdf)

1. Dating (Social customs) – Anecdotes – Comic books, strips,
etc. 2. Dating (Social customs) – Anecdotes. 3. Fans (Persons) –
Anecdotes – Comic books, strips, etc. 4. Fans (Persons) – Anecdotes.
5. Women – Anecdotes – Comic books, strips, etc. 6. Women – Anecdotes.
7. Sex – Anecdotes – Comic books, strips, etc. 8. Sex – Anecdotes.
9. Romance comic books, strips, etc. I. Nicholson, Hope, 1986-, editor

HQ801.S43 2015 646.7'7 C2015-906389-2
C2015-906390-6

Printed and bound in Canada

19 18 17 16 15 1 2 3 4 5

Table of Contents

Breather • *Sanya Anwar*   1

Platinum Funders   7

Introduction • *Hope Nicholson*   9

Foreword • *Trina Robbins*   11

Comics, Paper Dolls, Glasses, Contacts • *Margaret Atwood*   13

Minas Tirith • *Marguerite Bennett*   17

Settings • *ALB*   23

The Control Systems of Desire • *Cara Ellison*   28

Lungerella • *Stephanie Cooke, ill. Deena Pagliarello*   32

Anne of LINUX PINE • *Erin Cossar, ill. Kristen Gudsnuk*   39

Waxing Moon • *Meags Fitzgerald*   46

How Fanfiction Made Me Gay • *J.M. Frey*   51

A Divorcee's Guide to the Apocalypse • *Katie West, ill. Kristen Gudsnuk*   59

Cherry • *Cherelle Higgins, ill. Rachael Wells, col. Meaghan Carter*   66

Bemused • *Roberta Gregory*   76

Both Sides of the Table and Between the Sheets • *Janet Hetherington*   81

Babes on a Bike • *Jen Bartel*   89

Fanfiction, F/F, angst • *Tini Howard*   90

Cosplay Love • *Renee Nault*   96

URL > IRL • *Gita Jackson*   97

Shipping • *Jenn Woodall*   101

Levelling Up Your Dating Profile • *Loretta Jean*   107

Read: 1:19 am • *Jen Aprahamian*   112

Mashing our Buttons • *Soha Kareem*   117

Mechanism • *Meaghan Carter*   122

I'm Your Biggest Fan • *Adrienne Kress*   127

Yes, No, Maybe • *Megan Kearney*   133

How Fanfic From an American Girl
Captured an English Boy • *Megan Lavey-Heaton, ill. Isabelle Melançon*   138

They Bury You in White • *Laura Neubert*   143

A Different Kind of Fantasy Roleplay • *Brandy Dawley, ill. Leslie Doyle*   149

Nerd Love • *Irene Koh*   153

Giant-Sized Regrets • *Jess Oliver-Proulx*   158

Puzzled Over Pints • *Jen Vaughn, col. Jordyn Bochon*   162

4 Fictional Happy Endings • *Diana McCallum*   165

Ménage à 3/Sticky Dilly Buns • *Gisèle Lagacé/David Lumsdon, col. Shouri*   170

Ghost Stories • *Annie Mok*   180

There's Nothing Wrong, It Must be Love • *Diana McCallum*   185

Girls With Slingshots • *Danielle Corsetto*   189

Rise of the Late Bloomer • *Hope Nicholson, ill. Kristen Gudsnuk .*   193

None the Wiser • *Diana Nock*   198

Heard it Through the Grapevine • *Brandy Dawley*   204

Regards to the Goblin King • *Megan Kearney, col. Jordie Bellaire*   207

Never Kiss a Writer • *Alicia Contestabile*   212

My Partner is Really a Superhero • *Trina Robbins, ill. Jessica Paoli*   217

No Country For Old Mentors • *Soraya Roberts, ill. Melissa Kay*   220

Pop Culture Metaphor • *Fionna Adams and Jen Vaughn*   225

A Geek Girl Room of Your Own • *Crystal Skillman*   229

Kids These Days… • *Natalie Smith*   235

May I Admire You Again Today? • *Twiggy Tallant*   238

Montreal, 1993 • *Mariko Tamaki and Fiona Smyth*   243

Love in the Time of Ethernet: Geeks & LDR • *Natalie Zina Walschots*   248

A First • *Gillian G.*   254

The Vulcan in Me • *Emma Woolley*   259

Better Than Fiction • *Sarah Winifred Searle*   265

Popping the Heat Sink • *Sam Maggs, ill. Selena Goulding*   271

Biographies   275

Kickstarter Backers   277

Platinum Funders

These Kickstarter backers are our Platinum level sponsors. Thank you so much for all your support!

@librarian_lush
A.Harley
Adam Felling
Aislinn Luk
Alan Wood
Alessandra Balsano
Alex Lyle
Alexandria K White
Alicia N. Mitchell
Alison King
Alix Comeau
Alli Hope Archer
Allison King
Amanda Ravage
Amanda Beldo
Amanda R
Amanda Söderberg
Amaquieria
Amelia O'Leary
Ameliabrave
Amy Cuthbertson
Amy Goolsby
Amy Weiler
Ana Olivia Saldanha
Anastasia A.
Andrea J.
Andrea
    McSassypants
Andreas Flato
Andrew Gorshenin
Andy Grant
Angela Daurio
Angela Pusateri
Anne Price
Ariel Mosley
Aristedis
Ashley Beery
Ashley Turner
Atwood Boyd
Atwood Fan
August C. Bourré
Austin Ziegler
Beto Zaleta Jr.
Bonnie Seidel
Boris Roberto
    Aguilar
Brent Jans
Bri Lafond

Brian Johnson
Brian Valiquette
Brittany N Race
Brittany Hammond
Brittany Stone
Broderick H.
Bryan Khoo
C. Joshua Villines
C. V. Foster
Caitlin M Coblentz
Carla S. Goodrum
Catherine Pye
Chanel
Chantel Ember
    Lichty
Charlotte A. Clark
Chase Leipert
Chel
Chelsea M.
Chris de Castro
Chris Marquardson
Christina Williams
Christine Chien
Chung Juen
Chunk Kelly
Cindy Blood
Claire Wilgar
Clara Nigh
Conor Fleming
Courtney Morrison
Crojo
Crystal F
Crystal Sutherland
Dan O'Neill
Dani Palomino
Daniel Byrom
Daniel Laloggia
Daphne & Nelson
Daphne Boey
Darin Skutt
David Chuhay
David Ryan
David Walter
Dawn & Tracy W-W
Daxa Taank
Deb Fondren
Deb Taylor
Debborah Donnelly

Decklin Foster
Deidri Deane
Denitt Perez
Dennis Holmén
Dhainee Pfafflin
DianaMatronic
Dizzy Olive
Dom Richardson
Donato Sinicco, III
Dr. Roy Nir
    Lieberman
Dusty Higgins
E. Wohlman
Elena Maureen
    Martinez
Elizabeth
    Beauregard
Elizabeth Holz
Ellen Scherberth
Emily Peverall
Emily Spence Place
Emma B
Emma Woolley
Eric Neuhaus
Eric Pynnonen
Eric Whittaker
Erik & Dale Meyer-
    Curley
Erin Allison
    Stedman
Esther MacCallum-
    Stewart
Evan D Moore
Evan Schaeffer
Evonne Okafor
FadingSun32
Finn Upham
Fleur Mongan
Floppy J Cow
Gabe C.
Gabriel de los
    Angeles
Genevieve
    Starczewski
Gharabally
Gina Thornhill
girlinaboyhouse
Greg Morris

H. Yanoska
H.K. Shewnarain
Hafsa Alkhudairi
Hannah Fordham
Harald Demler
Harry Gunn
Hasnah Najla
Heather S.
Heidi Atwood
Hélène Deval
Hilary Craig
Hilary Mohs
Hillary Bowen
Ilona Rossman Ho
Ivan Bueno
Iván de Neymet
    Franco
Ivan Salazar
Jaclynn Scripps
Jacqueline Nichols
Jade Read
Jairus Khan
James Evans
James Kotsias
James Thomas
    Williams
Janna Solis
Jasmine Lammers
Jeanne Satre
Jennifer Dakki
Jennifer Davis
Jennifer K. Koons
Jennifer M. Sloane
Jennifer P. Wick
Jeremy D. Frens
Jessi Stone
Jesyka Bartlett
Jett Jones
Jewel Millard
Jill Adler
JL Piper
Joann M. Gomez
Joey Bajcar
Joey Chiu
Joey Tech
John Benson
Jolene Wong
Jon Linklater-

Johnson
Jon Newlands
Jonathan Ore
Jordana Greenblatt
Jules
Justin Herrick
Karl "Sycp" Dynes
Karla Hyde
Karyn Pinter
Kat H
Kate Kosturski
Katherine Long
Katherine Prevost
Kathryn Coyne
Kathryn Urbaniak
Kathy Trinh
Kathy Yi
Katie M. T. Crowell
Katie Pennell
Katrina M. Parra
Kelly Cassidy
Kendra Lynne
   Skowronnek
Keri Dawn
   Reininger
Keri Oleniach
Kim Hulslander
Kim mongoven
Kimberly McKinnis
Kitty Terban
Kj Weir
Kris Perez Webster
Kris Punke
Kris Roland
Krista Brandon
Kristin Evenson
   Hirst
Kristine Bolander
Krisztina Bunzl
L. Crabb
L. Park
LaShawna Covey
Lesley W
Lexie C.
Lili Koponen
Lily Mo
Lincoln Russell
Lindsay Smith
Lisa R. Nelson
Liwayway Piano
Liz Apollo
Luc de Chancenotte
Lucas Laib

M. C. Hawk
Macbeth Shawn
   Faguerson
Madeleine Fenner
Madeline
   Muntersbjorn
Madeline Zamoyski
Mama Jane
Marcel Jackwerth
Marek Lipták
Maria Bement
Maria Caporale
Marianne Kranz
Marie Benoit
   Ingram
Markus Magnitz
Mary Newsom
Matt
Matt Benter
Matthew
   Kirshenblatt
Matthia McCracken
Maureen Kennedy
Mayer Turkin
Megan Jessup
Megan McKenzie
Megan Redlawsk
Megan Struttmann
Megara
Melinda Cordero
Melissa Brown
   Sindler
Melissa House
Melissa Lehtonen
Merja
Micaela Gamboa
Micaela Suarez
Michael Gravely
Michael Handler
Michael Long
Michael Sean Miller
Michelle & Tianna
Mike Kauffman
Miranda Rhys-Jones
Mirra Neiman
Missy Kirtley
Mo Ormonde
MrMcGins
Mrs. Emily K. Arden
Nadia Mendez
Naomi Macleod
Nat Kisa "Kizna" A
Natalie B. Litofsky

NerdsCentral.com
Nicholas George
Nicholas Larzalere
Nicole Bamberger
Nicole Pin
Niki Dash
Nirakone Phromk-
   haranourak
Ohad Yankelevitch
Patricia Skermont-
   Pohrte
Paula Lee Phillips
Paula Paul
Peggy Hailey
Per Klitgaard
Kellie Brabec
Pilar Starr
   DeLaTierra
Qaantar
R Bruce MacKeen
R. Headley
rc
Rebecca Diem
Rebecca Flaum and
   Aaron Tomb
Rebecca Gorgas
Ren Ama Mizu
Renee L. Antoine
Rhys N.H.
Richard Crossman
Rick Dalby II
Ricki Lee Hodges
Rissa Lyn
Robert Macmillan
Robert Riley-
   Mercado
Robert Rose
Robert Stradley
Robin Babe Draper
Robin H. Sommo
Ryan Troock
S F McGinley
S Galletly
Salvatore A Siena
Samantha Vavrik
Sara J. Stambaugh
Sara M. Dorchak
Sarah Day
Sari Boone
Scout Johnson
SD Gottlieb
Sean Hutchinson
Selene O'Rourke

Shae Ciel Bendell
Shelby Logsdon
Sheree
   Christoffersen
Skip Olney
Skye Wathen
Sleepy Warlord
SOWEN <3!
Stephanie Gerk
Stephanie Hamilton
Stephanie Rozek
Stephen Graham
Stephen O. Wong
Stephen Shiu
Steve Leger
Steve Tilley
Steve Tornes
Stryker & River
Susan Damon
Suzy Metaxas
Sylvain
Terri Zagst
Tessa Baughman
Tiina Uusi-Rasi
Tina Whitley
Todd Good
Tom B
Tori McConnell
Tracie Armendariz
Travis and Vivienne
Valgerður Ása
   Kristjánsdóttir
Vanessa Cartwright
Victoria Chinn
Victoria Livingston
Virginia
W F Jackson
Wei Jiun Lim
Wendy Runyon
Yinka "KP" Adeniji
Yuki Tanaka
Zackary Downey
Zoe Lewycky

Introduction

Hope Nicholson

Why did I feel this book needed to be made?

I have a simple answer, this needed to get made because this was the type of book I wanted to read. That's that. I like talking to my friends about our romantic worries and successes, and I thought maybe you would like to hear their stories too. And as someone who consumes a LOT of media, I never get to see these stories on TV, in books, in comics, or on film, except on very rare occasions.

If you're holding this in your hand, you must agree!

There's an element in this question though, and one that is often asked after, that I've been perplexed on how to answer.

How is romance for fangirls different than for non-fangirls?

In short, it's not. The same problems that face fangirls with love are those that every person, regardless of gender or interest, has to deal with. Do they like me? Do I like them? Am I weird? What do I do?

And this book is not an answer to that. Sorry! That's something that everyone has to figure out on their own. Even if it's just figuring out that it will always be an unknown.

The one thing that characterizes fangirls though, is an obsession, a fixation, a passion, for the worlds that have been created outside of the one we live in. For many of us, we learn to understand ourselves through these worlds. For so many people out there, a fictional crush is just as intense as a real-world one, and a whole hell of a lot safer! (For me, it was Trent from Daria. Swoon.)

In this book, we've turned this obsession with fandom inwards, analyzing ourselves and how we relate to the world, and how that world is reflected back at us. It was important to me to have stories from a variety of experiences. Who we are, and how we identify ourselves at any given moment (and which is often subject to change throughout our lives!), affects our stories as much as the circumstances that surround us. In this collection we have storytellers from a variety of backgrounds, of all different ages (16-78), careers (writers, artists, coders, strippers, mechanics, journalists), ethnicities, sexualities (bi, pan, straight, gay), relationship status (single, married, polyamorous, monogamous), and desire levels (high sex-drives, demisexuals). These are women telling stories about their love lives, maybe about a specific moment they had that stuck with them, an idea about dating they've been dwelling on, or how they noticed love and sex in their favourite fandom.

I know you'll enjoy these stories, and I hope it starts off some fascinating conversations about the myriad ways we each experience love, sex, and dating.

Foreword

Trina Robbins

There have always been geeky girls. Marie Curie was one. ("Marie, get your nose out of that book and fix your hair! Pierre will be calling on you in 15 minutes! That girl, she'll never find a husband!") (But she did.) Ada Lovelace was another.

I was a geeky girl years before anybody had heard of computers (Well, except for Ada Lovelace), much less *Star Wars* or *Dungeons & Dragons*. But there were comics, and there was science fiction! I was a geek because I read science fiction, and nobody else in my 1950s high school did. Even my beloved sister thought I was weird, and laughed at the notion of men on Mars (for some reason, it was never women on Mars.)

If reading science fiction didn't make me geeky enough, I also had no idea how to be a normal teenage girl. All those popular girls seemed to have been born with a knowledge that I lacked. They knew how to talk to guys and they dated football players. They must have taught makeup on a Jewish holiday at my predominantly Catholic high school, so I missed it and as a result didn't know the difference between Max Factor and Maybelline. But I did know that B.E.M. stood for Bug-Eyed Monster!

Eventually I met two other teenage science fiction fans, both boys: David and Marty. We would hang out in David's furnished basement where his father had installed a ping pong table in hopes that his son might turn out to be normal. None of us ever used the ping pong table, but we did a lot of raiding David's refrigerator for cokes and arguing the respective merits of Arthur C. Clarke and Ray Bradbury.

David and Marty introduced me to EC Comics. I wasn't too crazy about the horror titles, but I loved *Weird Fantasy* and *Weird Science*, because they adapted Ray Bradbury stories, and especially *Mad Magazine. Mad* taught me to question authority, and ultimately was responsible for me becoming a hippie.

Because I was the only girl science fiction fan in all of Queens, David developed a crush on me. He was kind of a lumbering guy with an unfortunate flat piggy face, and to make matters worse, he was a freshman while I was a sophomore, so I would try to avoid being seen with him as he trailed after me in the halls, books piled up in his arms, loose papers flying behind him. But after school, hanging out in his basement, I was nice as could be, and David somehow forgave me.

In 1969, when I finally sat in front of a television set with my sister, watching men (Still not women!) really walking on the moon, I felt so *justified!* ("See? See? I told you!")

In the end, the geeky girls win. Eventually the popular girls in my high school married their football players and had a house in the suburbs and 2½ kids. But I and Ada Lovelace and Marie Curie – and all the geeky girls in this book – scorned no longer, write books, draw comics, play with computers, and have the time of our lives.

Although I never did figure out how to put on makeup.

Comics

Margaret Atwood

Paper Dolls

Margaret Atwood

Glasses

Margaret Atwood

Contacts

Margaret Atwood

Minas Tirith

Marguerite Bennett

i

Sansa Stark loves lemon cake, and so does the girl I love.

ii

Tell me a story.

And we're lying in bed with a Yankee Candle burning and the scent of lemon cake filling up the tiny rented room. New York thunders and drones and rolls outside, rattling wheels and squealing traffic, the weight of night settling down over the city, like wet cotton. In the dark of the room, her eyes shine back at me, mirrors to the flame.

In a hole in the ground, there lived a hobbit, I begin, and she sinks her teeth, teasing, against my shoulder.

I never got into Lord of the Rings *much*, she says. *The elves and dwarves and swords and castles, and everything had a name, had a backstory – had to keep looking at the map at the front –*

This map? I ask, pressing her back, so her chest turns, warm with sleep, to the dark ceiling and the flickering light. She laughs. She lets me.

I run my hand down the plain between her breasts. My clicking nails become swift horses, drumming over the heat of her skin, and I murmur in her ear.

Here, I say, kissing her left breast, *here is Minas Tirith, and the throne of the realms of men –*

And softly drumming my nails across the steppes of her skin to the other –

And here is Minas Morgoth, where Sauron watches. The pads of my fingers, tracing veins, like rivers. *Sister cities, the light and the dark.*

Why is this Minas Tirith? she whispers, and pinches the citadel-tip of one breast until it stings, red and rising, glowing with heat as the tower of Gondor would have gleamed with the glare of the sun.

That's the good city, I say.

Why good? she asks.

Because, I tell her, and bend my mouth to her breast, *it's over your heart.*

iii

Saturday morning, and it's raining hard in Brooklyn. Long blue curtains of rain sweep and surge and sweep again; we can't tell the thunder from the roar of the L train. I stand behind her in the kitchen, her back against my chest, her hands within my hands, and I am showing her how to slide the tips of her lovely long thumbnails into the flesh of a ripe fig. My fingers run over her fingers, and she's giggling as we split it open, unfolding it gently back, until inside she sees the secrets of it, all soft and sugar-sweet, the seeds like a smile, like tiny pearls.

Put your tongue, here. My voice in her ear, the fig in her hands, in my hands, worlds within worlds within worlds. *Try to imagine where these grew – try to imagine how long people have been eating these, all the way back through history... before chocolate, before candy, Greek and Roman, Carthage and Phoenicia, all the way back, these tumbling fat and ripe down into your hands –*

You sound like Hannibal Lecter, she grins. She kisses me, sugar-lipped, teeth like seed pearls.

And you taste like Will Graham, I add.

She bites me now. I kiss her again, letting her push me against the wall, letting her sticky fingers run the line of my cheek, letting her bite, and kiss, and suck, and bite again – letting her devour me, as the L train runs on through the rain.

iv

Wand? she asks, twitching her feet in my lap, so I might better massage her aching heels. Cosplay has its consequences, but you never saw a more beautiful Batgirl on the streets of Gotham.

Apple and phoenix feather, I tell her. *Long. I'm like nine feet tall.*

Yes you are, O Amazon.

I'm more Kate Kane than Wonder Woman, I remind her, working up the monkeyish joints of her toes. *Well-intentioned. Selfish. What's your wand?*

Cherry and maybe dragon heartstring. She pours the rest of the champagne into my glass. *Rich and dark. Devoted. Your House?*

Clean split, Hufflepuff and Slytherin, I answer. *I'm the den mother to all the cunning ambitious types. Socialite of supervillains. You?*

Gryffindor, in it to win it. No compromise of morals. No distractions.

What's your Patronus? I ask, and it seems strange that I have not asked until now.

These are the questions that matter more, more than how many siblings we have, than what our parents do for a living, than what television shows we follow in the fall. What is your Patronus? What is the thing that represents all protection to you, all reassurance, all strength, all love? What is the happiest moment you can remember, to summon the spell to you? What drives away the dark in your heart?

Probably some big cat, she says, playing with her batarang. *You may pet me and feed me and worship me on my terms and absolutely mine alone, and if you touch my fluffy, fluffy belly, I'm taking your hand.*

She curls her toes around my probing fingers. *I'm* also *going to sit in your lap while you're trying to write.*

I arch my eyebrow at her, failing not to smile. *I would get very little writing done. In the words of the scholars and poets, my dove... 'O, dat ass.'*

She giggles. Her con badge lies on the coffee table – once the thing on which so much hinged – coveted, protected, sought after, the passport to everything desired, the Hogwarts letter – but now that the con is over, no more than a cut of plastic. Muggle foolishness.

Mine is... a fox, I answer, trying to make this sound a light thing. When I was younger, the nature of my Patronus was as inconstant as a child's daemon – sometimes arctic wolves, for my parents, or sometimes the person I loved – a bloody tiger, a polar bear. Some were ideals I had in my head – a stag peppered with arrows, or a golden eagle, shrieking and raw. But I am older now, and I am come far from the girl who would cry out for a rescue.

A fox, yes. My Patronus is the same as my Animagus. Just – me.

That's definitely the most Marguerite thing I've heard in awhile.

I run the knuckle of my finger up her foot and she arches her back luxuriantly.

I get by, I tell her.

Foxes for... duality, she breathes. *You told me this, I think.*

My throat hitches unexpectedly, unsure of how much I want to say, of how pretentious it will all sound. It's idle fangirl chatter, yes, but it is secrets, too, knowledge more intimate than you would care to make known to strangers. Would you trust a stranger to know what you saw in the Mirror of Erised? Would you trust a stranger to know what shape the boggart in the wardrobe would take, for you?

This kind of self-awareness is valuable, I say, mild as Lupin. *We don't have touchstones in common lore and folktales so much. We have fandom.*

Foxes are... all kinds of things, I say, working up the tendon of her foot. *Flirting vixen, anxious scavenger. Aesop's trickster – the one who longed for the Little Prince to tame her. Chicken killer, plague bringer. When you domesticate them, did you know they wag their tails and their ears get floppy?*

Predator and prey, she says. She doesn't mind that I talk like a novel.

What memory would you use? she asks, shutting her eyes. *To summon your Patronus, I mean.*

I pause. I wasn't expecting this question.

The night... the night Scott Snyder asked me to write Batman *with him.*

Her eyes open. *Wait, no kidding?*

Yeah. I look down at her feet in my lap, her blue toenail polish. *Pulled me aside after class...It was January, and it was so, so cold...There was snow on the ground, and the dark...just...On the drive home, I had to pull over onto the side of the road and screw up my eyes and stare at the ceiling to keep myself from crying. I just thought over and over, 'I'm saved, I'm saved. I don't have to go back South to the life and husband and future I don't want. Thank you, whatever's out there, for the gift of my life. I'm really, really just...I'm saved.'*

I stare at the blue of her toenails. I realize I've stopped stroking her. For no reason at all, I feel like crying.

What memory would you use? I ask quietly, to cover the silence.

She looks out the window, at the snow.

Maybe this one, she says. *Tonight, here, with you.*

v

The whole thing was my fault, in the end. They're usually my fault, in the end. I was the one to send her away. I fall in love with the story I write on the girl. I neglect the girl. I lose the girl. In that inevitable, unenviable end, I am left with only a story – the story I did not want, but the story I deserve – the story I have earned.

vi

We saw each other at a party some time ago.

Nerds in the city, in Bushwick, a Friday night marathon, moths in the streetlamps and crocuses in the flowerbeds. There was Magic: The Gathering in one room, Dungeons & Dragons in another, and on the flat screen in the grad school den –

The Fellowship of the Ring.

She was there with her boyfriend.

He does not talk like a novel. He does not write stories that he loves more than girls who love him.

There was wine, and there was beer, and there were cocktails with clever names. There were cocktail dresses, cocktail questions – which, in this crew, came down to what House, what wand, what place on the Enterprise – what king, in the war for the Iron Throne.

And when someone asked – someone always asks – she told them that the memory for her Patronus was the night she met the boy she loved.

And as much as I wish I could rewrite myself, rewrite my story, make my own memory to summon the spell become the night that I knew she was finally happy – it would be a lie.

I am only ever half-tamed. And the happiest moment of my life was the moment I knew I could be free. Riding my selfishness, my ambition, my stories, ever to the ends of the earth, ever from the dark and the cold.

vii

We are friends still, for the curious. Still we speak in stories.

I am glad her boy is a Ravenclaw. I am glad he prefers Alana Bloom. I am glad he never read *The Hobbit*, and knows *Star Wars* better than *The Lord of the Rings*. I send her postcards from California, of movie sets, of Disneyland – of the life my ambition has bought me.

But that night, in Bushwick, as the movie played out in the other room, I knew what words were coming.

I peeled myself from the wall in the den. I went into the skinny railroad kitchen.

Alone in the dark, I stared at the fandom trappings of a stranger's life, a life neither hers nor mine. There was no lemon cake here, frosted, under glass. There were no figs on the windowsill. There were *Doctor Who* magnets, ice cube trays like Starfleet badges, and though I was the one who left, who ran, through some trick of the halls, still, the voices from the film followed me.

Boromir, abject and doubting, murmured of Minas Tirith.

Have you ever seen it, Aragorn? The White Tower of Ecthelion, glimmering like a spike of pearl and silver, its banners caught high in the morning breeze. Have you ever been called home by the clear ringing of silver trumpets?

Aragorn's soft voice came in answer. *I have seen the White City, long ago...*

And Boromir again, voice bright with longing, more than hope. *One day, our paths will lead us there...*

And as I stood in the dark of a stranger's kitchen with my eyes closed, my head tilted back, I saw Minas Tirith, rising like a sword of silver in the dawn.

I remember the dark and the flame and the music of the city as her heartbeat in my ear, the joy of the city as my hand, curved and soft as I lay dreaming peaceful in the shadow of her arms. I think of the breast of the girl I loved, falling asleep with my hair in whorls of gold across her chest, wishing I had the strength to guard her, to keep her, to be worthy to defend the realms of men.

vii

I loved her better because of the stories that she showed me.

I loved her best because of the stories that we shared.

These things, I remember.

The breath of the city, her voice in my ear, saying my name, my name, saying again and again, and, laughing, pleading,

A story –

Tell me a story.

you said
after bedtime,
you turned
all of your
notifications
off.
Settin
it's important
you'd say,
to separate yourself from technology. your brain needs to shut down properly.

but whenever I'd
text you late
at night,
I'm sorry. I know you're sleeping.
I'm just freaking out.. what if I can't do this?
what if I'm not strong enough
my love
you'd call.

I finally figured out that your rule applied to everyone,
I didn't mean to bother you...

are you ok?
no, I really need you right now..
I'm here. I'm here
except me.
xo ALB

The Control Systems of Desire

Cara Ellison

Probably sometime during the waiting, in the spring when I was being stacked with failure, instead of being released, I broke. People often wondered why I was waiting, and I couldn't tell them but for the fact of pure, chemical rush, the sort you get from releasing an arrow on some virtual feral animal, the thick, dull sound, 'thwp', like biting someone else's lip. To become the action associated with buttons. To become the touched. The roughly handled. The reward system itself. The adored items. The vista over the emerald cliff down to the sparkling lakes below. Just once, have someone else decide. I've always been this confident, passionate person who is in control, but he knew that I needed someone to press me down and fuck me until we lost the ability to think in words.

It is fall outside in America, but in a lush digital south Asian locale, he directs a deep-voiced protagonist to drive a jeep, recklessly scarring dirt tracks, stalking fascist insurgents through fictional country, creeping up on enemies and suffocating them with sinewy virtual arms. Some of the time the terse freedom fighter will hunt exotic animals, he upgrades abilities to hunt, fight, gather. Videogames always were a ground on which to study my own feelings for men.

The promise of everything, as we look down over the cliff, seems as broad as the map, the horizon stretching into the back of the TV. Role-playing games, where you often strip your environment of resources to upgrade and refashion your character into a better one, encourage patience because of the promises the systems suggest.

I sit trembling with anticipation, next to a person I am developing delicate, excruciating feelings for like watching the hot mess of sunrise soak upward, a person who may never give me what I want, who never expresses a need for anything from me, watching them play this first person role-playing videogame, wondering why I am so afraid of the mere inch of upholstery between us and suffering some awful desire that manifests like flu.

At some point past bedtime at the shore of the other person's chest, I realised that I was waiting to be the game itself, to be the systems that were worked, to be worthy of the kind of rapt attention that meant that I could say all the things that I wanted to say, that sitting there for hours without touching or kissing was torture, that being unable to hold someone who is right there is horror, that being patient – patience does not come naturally to someone who plays games for a living – being patient, oh, it is not my way, I cannot, just cannot wait, I need my reward now and not later. Staring at some five o'clock shadow in some deep dark cold suburb, I knew I wanted that warm couch to be the only virtual world and I wanted to be listened to as if there were a mission timer on my words.

Instead he smiled quietly. With all the calculations of a glinting arrow eased back on beautifully-rendered bow string, we both waited.

In games the work is often hollow. By the time you have reached the cap on upgrades, made the sumptuous-looking ensemble you wanted, you understand those hours have led to no lasting gain, just something shallow like a one night stand, perhaps sometimes the promise of a narrative kickback that you can relate to a drinking buddy before you restart. And now I am sitting here writing to you like we are in a pub, relating to you the story of how longing has collapsed my feelings into a coagulated mess, the dissatisfaction I feel with most games mirrored in them.

Want is this awful thing that you know you should not have or let rule you, but it can gouge a hole in you.

A game is a thing and not a person, but there are rules too in real life between people: you can't ask the other person what they really want from you until about three months in, and if you see them less than once a week probably longer. In the end, a lot of the time, the answer is "I don't know." Looking at this problem from a designer's point of view, you avoid ever making a game where you don't know what you want from the player, because then the player loses interest. The attention is applied elsewhere.

I can't stop thinking about the promise that videogames play on. The idea that if I were good enough, the ending would be spectacular, enthralling, happy. That if I played the whole game perfectly, moulding parts of myself around the other person and what they needed, I'd be a better person too.

I am learning not to want or to compromise. To never boot up a game in case I have to spend time on it. The time I invested in most games, at least as a critic, was time that I wished back, and only rarely found the one who wanted to spend time on me. At some point, maybe I should admit that my beloved videogames are used to distract us from life. They are a way to avoid telling people how hopeless we feel.

I guess I was scared of the space between me and him, because all the other men gradually, slowly, painfully betrayed my investment, and to show how much you desperately want something is a weakness and a failure. Wanting is something that only women who are ugly, untalented and hysterical do. You must accept the game you are given. If you have to play it like a man to seem aloof, well.

Keep your hands on the controller. Murder your emotions.

I lie under the smothering duvet of my childhood single bed in a kind of limbo. As a very young child I had a less sophisticated form of favourite game, those plastic tile puzzles where you slide the jumbled tiles around to reveal the picture. This particular one, found in a cereal box, and even in a jumbled state clearly depicting the Disney character Pluto, was soothing to play, in a haptic sense. To grind those tiles over and over again, to click them into place and 'solve' the puzzle of the picture, only to become unsatisfied with the results. As a kind of meditation, I think now about sliding those tiles. No matter what I did, the 'reward' of the picture being 'revealed' was not quite as satisfying as sliding those tiles around. Of playing.

The 'solution' was in itself unattainable because whatever you did, there was always that last square, a hole, in the picture. The mere idea that there was still a hole in the picture meant it was never finished. There was no closure. You are just moving the gap around.

Sometimes you can play perfectly, and still, you cannot have what you want.

Lungerella

Stephanie Cooke, illustrations by Deena Pagliarello

Once upon a time of technological wonders, there lived a girl named Lungerella. Lungey, as she was called, lived quietly in the woods with her parents where they were super basic. They lived simply, without distractions such as TV or videogames.

When Lungey was not playing with the other kids, she often sat under her favourite tree and pondered life. She wondered whether or not she would ever find true love. She dreamt of finding a tall, dark and handsome stranger and their history together would begin the moment that they locked eyes. Lungey thought a lot about this. She had a lot of time on her hands. Like I said, she was basic.

When Lungey wasn't otherwise preoccupied, her favourite thing to do was to read. She could get absorbed in a book for hours at a time and not even realize how many minutes had flown by. Lungey consumed book after book.

On a particularly beautiful day, as Lungey was reading, you know, under her favourite tree, a boy spotted her and approached her.

"Lungey, why do you bother with books? You ain't gonna need them to raise kids!" he said.

Unable to muster a response, she stared at him, completely appalled. She knew she had to find people who appreciated her as she was.

Years went by and Lungerella's love for books had not dissipated. In fact, her love had grown and now included manga, comics, videogames, movies and more. She had friends and people that she could share her passions with and life was pretty great. Lungey was happy.

However, there was something missing from her life: romance. She had put off trying to find someone because she had other things in her life that made her happy. She knew that she didn't need a man and while she wasn't lonely, she longed to find someone that she connected with on a deeper level, beyond friendship.

It was hard to meet new people. Lungey had given up a life of easy jobs to freelance, which meant long hours at home with little connection to the outside world. She wasn't a hermit, but her social circle was limited. Lungey decided to resolve her problem and came to a simple conclusion: take the process to the Internet where dating sites existed in vast quantities. That night Lungey created a profile for herself and began the search for Mr. Right.

First there was Spindr, a site that allowed Lungey to look at basic information and a photo to decide whether or not she might be interested. She liked the concept and was pleasantly surprised by the number of attractive men that seemed to occupy it. She swiped right for a number of men that she could see herself going on a date with. For every gem there were several duds but the ratio seemed to be delivering decent prospects.

Lungey began to feel like maybe the whole dating thing wasn't so bad and pondered why she hadn't thought to try this sooner.

She began conversations with her prospective dates. SlapShot83 was her favourite of the initial batch. He answered quickly and seemed to have a great grasp of the English language for someone who professionally played hockey and regularly got pucks to the head.

Just as Lungey received a text from a friend reading "Be careful on Spindr, it's a zoo!" she received a notification from SlapShot83.

With a smile, she opened up the message and her smile immediately faded away. Attached to the message was an image of what she initially assumed was a melting popsicle and then realized that she had been messaged a photo of a mostly flaccid penis. With a look of disgust, she texted her friend back with details of what had just transpired, ending her message with, "Why would anyone send a photo of a flaccid penis? That's like taking a photo of a sunrise at 3 pm!"

With that, Lungey deactivated her profile.

Next, Lungey decided to try StupidCupid. She downloaded the app to her phone and created a profile with the username "hellarella."

Within moments of making her profile public, responses started to flood in. Some people would just ping her to let her know that they were interested while others would send messages, trying to convince her that they were worth her time.

Some messages were simple, containing just "hello" or "hi" or "how are you?" while others were more fun such as "Would you rather go on a date with Batman or Superman?" and played to her geeky interests. Those messages were the ones she enjoyed responding to, even if she didn't find the person sending them particularly attractive. There was just something about a good question that lured her in. She liked that strangers could do that to her simply based on some info in a profile.

Lungey wondered how anyone introverted managed to find love before the Internet existed. The mere thought of anyone saying any of

these things to her in person gave her massive anxiety and caused her face to turn beet red.

Lungey set up dates with three prospective men over the course of the following week.

Antony was the first of the three dates. Technically, Lungey had met him at a videogame store where they chatted and flirted on occasion, but nothing had come of it until Antony had found Lungey on StupidCupid. He took the opportunity to message her and formally ask her on a date, which she accepted. Antony wasn't the Prince Charming that Lungey had in mind but it was clear that the two of them already had quite a bit in common.

The date wasn't terrible, but Antony made it really clear right off the bat that he was looking for someone to commit to on a long-term basis. During the first portion of their date, he listed the numerous members of the family that she would have to meet over the next little while, causing Lungey's chest to tighten.

After Lungey's date with Antony, he began to text her relentlessly. She'd had a nice time with him but there was just no spark. She had no desire to play out the situation and decided it was best to be straight with him. Lungey texted him her farewells.

> **LUNGEY:** *I had a good time on our date, but I just didn't feel any fireworks with us. You're really sweet but I don't think we should see each other again.*
> **ANTONY:** *Where is this coming from?! Why would you do this to us? Why would you do this to YOU?! I KNOW you were happy with me! I could FEEL it! You were SO HAPPY!"*
> **LUNGEY:** *Well, we had fun, but I just don't see this going anywhere so I'm sorry but I think it's better if we just move on and move forward.*
> **ANTONY:** *We need to talk about this! Why are you forsaking your future?!*

Lungey couldn't believe it. Was this the sort of thing that happened when you tried to be honest and up-front? She sighed and decided to go to sleep for the night and hope that the morning brought less crazy.

Lungey's second date was with Phil. They hit it off online and chatted endlessly about videogames and board games. After a couple days of banter, they set a date to meet up. Lungey suggested a new board game café that had just opened up and felt pretty proud when Phil seemed genuinely pleased with her decision.

Board games were played and as the evening unfolded, Lungey found herself enjoying Phil's company. Inevitably the night had to come to an end and the time came to settle up at the café. Like a gentleman, Phil paid for the outing and blushing, Lungey thanked him. As they walked out, Lungey suddenly realized that she didn't have an exit strategy and panic set in. "How do you end a date?!" she internally screeched. Lungey began to slow her pace as her mind raced, "Do I hug him? Do we kiss on the first date? Did we even have a connection worth kissing over? Do I shake his hand? What if he invites me back to his place? WHAT DO I DO?!"

They walked to the corner of the street where Lungey informed Phil that her streetcar would be by any moment. They smiled at each other, which led Lungey to panic and to raise her right hand and shout "HIGH FIVE!" at a stunned Phil who had no other option than to reciprocate the awkward gesture. Cringing, Lungey rushed away to the streetcar, which was thankfully in sight.

The rest of Lungey's evening revolved around tormenting herself and replaying the high-fiving incident in her head. She lay in bed and sighed into her pillow while her cat circled her hoping for some affection. "You and me are going to be stuck together forever," she told her beloved pet.

The third and final date of the week was with Jake. Lungey and Jake had hit it off and according to StupidCupid, were incredibly compatible. Jake took the initiative right off the bat to just make a date.

Lungey had learned that you could have chemistry with someone via text very easily but whether or not that translated into real life was an entirely different matter. It was another way that the Internet had changed dating.

Jake set the date for the following day at a coffee shop just down the street from Lungey. She arrived early, ordered a coffee and sat down with a book.

Shortly after the appointed time, Jake walked in and Lungey was taken aback by how cool and chill he seemed. Lungey had also learned quickly that people lie online about pretty much everything. If someone said that they were 5'9", they were probably actually 5'6". If a cute photo of someone seemed too good to be true, it probably was, but Jake was exactly as advertised. He was charming and cute and he clearly knew it, but it worked for him. Lungey was pleasantly surprised.

The date didn't take a turn for the worse and after some initial rambling and flailing, Lungey found a comfort zone somewhere in between quiet panic and content conversation. The pair talked for hours, exchanging stories and getting to know one another.

The end of the evening came too soon and the farewell brought something new to Lungey's life: a lack of anxiety. Almost as if they could read each other's mind, both Lungey and Jake looked at each other and acknowledged how much fun they'd had. From there, both realized that while they had really enjoyed each other's company, there hadn't been a spark between them. Jake walked Lungey home and asked if he could contact her again to hangout but just as friends. While Lungey hadn't planned on making a new friend, she was happy.

She knew there was no point in trying to force a relationship that neither of them felt and it seemed very adult to come to this decision.

After three dates, Lungerella hadn't found her Prince Charming but she wasn't deterred. The three dates, while not perfect, helped Lungey realize some of the things that she wanted in a person and some of the things that she didn't. She knew now to be open-minded and to not hunt down someone who solely shared her interests, she had learned that it was enough to find someone who didn't judge her for what she loved and didn't shut her down when she wanted to chatter endlessly about the latest comic book movie.

There were still good potential partners out there to be found. Even when nothing came from an interaction or a date, it helped her learn more about who she was and who she wanted to be on her own, and as someone's partner, and that made the whole process worth it.

PINE EMAIL SERVER

TO: HAN SOLO

I LIKE KURT VONNEGUT

FROM: HAN SOLO

MARRY ME

Anne of LINUX PINE

Erin Cossar, illustration by Kristen Gudsnuk

In 1996, I went to university and received my first-ever email
account: A school-assigned text-based PINE address that could only
be accessed in the email room and library from 7 am to 9 pm daily.
The terminals had single-colour monitors and it ran on LINUX. There
was, and this might seem quaint, absolutely no Internet in the dorms
whatsoever, and most people did not own computers. This was before
cell phones, text messaging, Facebook, online dating, or swiping
right – digital communication was at its most rudimentary.

I am from an isolated, rural town on the east coast and was eager to
get out of Heather Chandlerville and find other well-read, alternachick
Veronica Sawyers with weird interests. Sure, there were a few kindred
souls in my hometown, but for the most part, I fielded constant
annoying commentary about how I looked, sounded, and acted
"different." Anyone who was the weird kid from their small town knows
exactly what I mean. If my friendship goals were a personal ad in the
student newspaper, it would have read "Girl obsessed with a) reading
b) punk and grunge and c) the Sci-Fi Channel seeks same. Must love
multiple-choice lists."

Immediately after moving into the dorms, I joyfully realized that
Veronica Sawyers were a) everywhere and b) also seeking same. I
quickly discovered a a bunch of girls whose tastes (in clothes, music,
TV, movies and books, among other things) intersected with mine in
a major way. They had already made friends with some of the second-

year guys, whom I then became friends with as well. I was suddenly plunged into a social circle where nobody thought my entertainment choices were weird – in fact, they were open to hearing about them – and I wasn't subject to constant reminders that my sartorial choices were strange. I actually swapped clothes with some of them.

I also harboured a secret fantasy about having an epistolary-novel romance littered with ten-cent words. This was a result of reading too many books about fulfilling pen-pal arrangements, including Anne Shirley's stint at Windy Poplars and the *Pen Pals* series by Sharon Dennis Wyeth. I had a soft spot for letters from boys. I'd had relationships during high school, but was ready for something different.

Six weeks into classes, I was in the email room with a Veronica we'll pseudonymously call Padme, clacking out PINE missives. I finished quickly and wanted to leave, so Padme scribbled down an email address on a piece of paper (so vintage!) belonging to a guy we'll call Han Solo, who was at another campus ten hours away. She thought we'd have a lot in common.

I humoured her by typing a single line to Han. I was sure it would dissolve into the ether with no response, because it was something that I'd started actively using to deflect people:

```
   PINE 3.92 COMPOSE MESSAGE REPLY        Folder: INBOX 8 Messages

TO           : Han Solo <hansolo@mun.ca>
Cc           :
Attchmnt     :
Subject      : Hi
-----Message Text -----

I like Kurt Vonnegut.
```

At that point, Vonnegut references had received a 99% response rate of "Who?" I forgot about it until the next day when I received another single line in reply:

```
Subject      : RE: Hi
-----Message Text -----

Will you marry me?
```

Han and I started to email back and forth wildly during 7 am and 9 pm. Our interests intersected: music, books, television, pop culture, and – a novelty for me – science fiction. We talked about Vonnegut, the meaning of lyrics, *Star Wars* – and he managed to weave flirtation into discussion of said interests. His incredible sense of humour featured a quick, sarcastic wit. We eventually started trading phone calls, me on the pay phone in the dorm hallway.

```
-----Message Text -----
Way back in 1996, f65erc wrote:
> This is sudden. I take it you're a Vonnegut fan?

I've never met anyone else who was into Vonnegut. I thought I
should do a pre-emptive strike. My favourite is God Bless You,
Mr. Rosewater. If you've never read it, you can borrow mine.
```

I was completely smitten, level: Dwayne Hoover with Kilgore Trout.

```
teaching a Vonnegut book, but alas, the class was full.

Way back in 1996, hansolo wrote:
> Cool beans. But if I did manage to clone myself, I wouldn't
> let the other clones near you. I don't need the competition.

You're rating high on the Exile in Guyville Flower scale right
now: a) obnoxious b) funny c) true and d) mean. See: Phair, Liz
```

And technically, we were "online dating." Just before that was a household word.

I didn't realize that what I liked most about corresponding through email – that it was a filter I could use to carefully present a polished, more palatable version of myself, something sociologists call "impression management" – would also be its worst feature.

I privately considered Han my boyfriend, although I'd never said that out loud to anyone, even to the Veronicas, although they could tell just how into him I was, and I had a Bantha-sized pile of hopes and expectations about where this was leading.

However, a few weeks later, Veronica-Padme sent me a message via email, even though we were sitting in the same room:

```
-----Message Text -----
I've got something to tell you, and you're not going to like it.
```

Then she turned to me and told me about the email she'd just gotten from Han. She said he'd gone to a party the night before and slept with someone else. He just wanted casual sex, but now the girl seemed to want more. Padme also told me she thought Han was trying to get back together with his ex-girlfriend, who had dumped him. He had told me it was a "mutual split" (it's never mutual – whoever says that is the dumpee).

I went back to my room, curled into a small ball on the tiny bed, and cried. This was something I shouldn't have known, but I did know and couldn't un-know. I was hurt, and furious. But the thing was...I really had no right to be angry about it.

Because I was seeing someone else too.

On campus, I was dating someone we'll call Luke, also a friend of Padme. Han knew Luke – they had grown up in the same town, gone to high-school together and both were in the same social circle as Padme.

I am definitely a monogamist. I have no interest in dating more than one person at a time. Yet I was. I cherry-picked all the Luke bits out of my correspondence with Han, and in turn didn't mention Han to Luke, pushing any guilt or consideration of what was right, wrong, or fair deep into the back of my mind. The amount of dissonance between my actions and my beliefs was staggering, so I really had nothing to do with all of my resentment and hurt feelings except to swallow them. Part of me felt Han should have told me he was seeing other people. But how could I think that, when I was openly dating Luke and people referred to us as a couple?

I kept corresponding with Han, although I became passive-aggressive and distant. A few days later, things got even more absurd when I found out that Luke actually had a long-term girlfriend of six years – at 18, six years is the temporal equivalent of a silver anniversary – who was at university in another province. Everyone, including the Veronicas, kept telling me the same thing over and over:

```
-----Message Text -----
I thought you knew.
```

Fuck, no. I didn't. But they all thought I did – that Luke must have told me, or that it must have come up at some point – and that I was fine with it. I also learned Luke was a notorious a) womanizer and b) serial cheater. These were also things people had thought I was aware of, and I probably should have been – I was almost impossibly naive, although I did find it odd that several girls I didn't know had gone out of their way to corner me and ominously tell me to stay away from him.

So to recap, I pursued two guys, lying to both of them, while being lied to by each of them as they also pursued and/or had relationships with other people. We all managed to accomplish this without the aid of texting or Tinder, just the digital equivalent of letter-writing plus a pay phone.

We let ourselves believe that we mean well with the self-curation we do online (omitting information from our profiles to maintain privacy, posting only about positive things that happen to us) but it can be very self-serving (untagging photos, refusing to update your relationship status, or even creating secret profiles or email accounts). Similarly, I chose not to examine what I was doing, because I knew that within the parameters of the relationship I wanted to have and the behaviour I expected out of a partner, what I was doing was wrong. And it hurt like hell when I was on the receiving end.

People often hold technology responsible for infidelity. And sure, there were aspects of Han's personality I totally missed due to his self-editing, but there were a lot of things I chose to gloss over due to infatuation. For instance, I later found out a) he didn't like animals b) he had slept with most of his friends' longterm girlfriends and c) had a bit of a mean streak. But while things like Facebook, texting and email certainly make it easier for people (particularly lazy people!) to blur the boundaries of their relationships, it's still the people involved who are to blame.

I am responsible for the terrible choices I made.

As for me, Han and Luke...the end was just as messy as the rest. Me and Han met in person during our flirtation stage, and that was intense but went swiftly downhill into a confusing tangle of resentment, sniping, and indecision between the three of us, plus the people they each were seeing (making it, at the very least, a love septagon). Luke got dumped by his girlfriend (and told me it was a "mutual decision"). I eventually decided I wanted to be with Han, who then promptly ghosted me for the duration of that summer, breaking my heart. I had already enrolled in a school in Han's town, so when I moved there in the fall, we ended up just repeatedly hooking up, ending with my heart broken for a second time. My Veronicas were there through all of that, and they never made me feel judged for my questionable behaviour. They also never judged the guys, which I now realize is at the crux of what real friends do for each other.

I think I found it so difficult to let go because it was something new to be involved with someone who openly had passionate, geeky interests, many of which intersected with mine. It added an extra dimension to dating that immediately became a non-negotiable for me. This was also when I learned to let go of the idea of relationships being tidy and beautiful like the ones in books. Messy is okay and is going to happen in adult relationships, especially if you choose to engage in relationships with a lot of moving parts. Also, remember the girl Han hooked up with at that party? We ended up meeting in person. She was a) artistic b) awesome and c) a total Veronica. We are still the best of friends.

Waxing Moon

MEAGS FITZGERALD

CARRIE* WAS MY SIXTH GRADE BEST FRIEND.

CARRIE

ME,
WITH A "COOL" HAIRCUT THAT MADE EVERYONE MISTAKE ME FOR MY BROTHER.

WE LOVED THE SAME THINGS,

PRACTICING OUR SLOW DANCE SKILLS,

I WANT TO STAND WITH YOU ON A MOUNTAIN,
I WANT TO BATHE WITH YOU IN A SEA **

STAGING OLD TIMEY PHOTOS,

35mm CAMERA

ONE OF MY MOM'S OLD BRIDESMAID DRESSES

AND WATCHING

SAILOR MOON

WE DEVOTEDLY WATCHED THE SHOW, COLLECTED THE STICKERS, TRADED THE CARDS AND DRESSED UP AS THE SAILOR SCOUTS FOR HALLOWEEN.

MY BEDROOM WAS SO THOROUGHLY LINED WITH SAILOR MOON POSTERS THAT THEY FUNCTIONED AS EXTRA INSULATION.

* NAME HAS BEEN CHANGED

** LYRICS TO SAVAGE GARDEN'S "TRULY MADLY DEEPLY"

THAT YEAR WE GOT THE INTERNET AT MY HOUSE.

wwi-wwo-wwi-ting-ting-tinng- shwa-shwa
shwa-breeeeee- breeeeee-kaking-kaking-
.shwa-breeeeee- breeeeee-kaking-kaking-
ppp-chchchch-CHCHCH-FFCHFFCHFFCH

Address: http://www.sailormercuryfanclub.net

I DIDN'T KNOW WHAT A SEARCH ENGINE WAS, SO I JUST GUESSED AT SOME SAILOR MOON URLS AND FOUND SITES BY TRIAL AND ERROR.

I LOVED FINDING PHOTOS FROM THE UNCENSORED, ORIGINAL JAPANESE VERSION OF THE SHOW. I DEVELOPED MONK-LIKE PATIENCE WHILE IMAGES LOADED.

1 MINUTE 3 MINUTES 5 MINUTES 7 MINUTES

IT'S MY TURN ON THE COMPUTER! I WANNA PLAY MINESWEEPER!

SISTER SPEAKING

HUNNY YOU HAVE TO GET OFF THE INTERNET, I NEED THE PHONE TO CALL GRANDMA.

MOM SPEAKING

CARRIE WAS AN ONLY CHILD. I LIKED GOING TO HER PLACE. IT WAS QUIET AND THERE WERE FANCY, FRAGILE THINGS EVERYWHERE. THEY DIDN'T HAVE INTERNET BUT THEY DID HAVE A CD-ROM ENCYCLOPEDIA.

DOES IT HAVE AN ENTRY FOR SAILOR MOON?

LET ME SEE. . . . NOPE.

WELL, WHAT ELSE SHOULD WE SEARCH FOR?

. . .

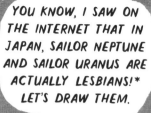

YOU KNOW, I SAW ON THE INTERNET THAT IN JAPAN, SAILOR NEPTUNE AND SAILOR URANUS ARE ACTUALLY LESBIANS!* LET'S DRAW THEM.

REALLY?!!!

WELL THEY CAN'T BE PART OF THIS COMPETITION BECAUSE LESBIANS CAN'T BE SEXY, BECAUSE LESBIANS DON'T HAVE SEX.

ARE YOU SURE?

YEAH DUH, IN THE ENCYCLOPEDIA IT SAID SEX IS DONE WITH A PENIS AND VAGINA, AND THERE'S NO PENIS, SO..?

*IN THE ENGLISH DUBBING THE RELATIONSHIP WAS CHANGED FROM LOVERS TO COUSINS.

I WASN'T CONVINCED. SO PRIVATELY, I STARTED MAKING DRAWINGS TO FIGURE OUT THE KINDS OF SEXY THINGS TWO WOMEN COULD DO TOGETHER.

3" BINDER FULL OF MY SAILOR MOON DRAWINGS.

SECRET COMPARTMENT IN THE BACK FOR MY RISQUÉ DRAWINGS.

IT NEVER OCCURRED TO ME TO SEARCH THE INTERNET FOR THIS KIND OF THING.

How Fanfiction Made Me Gay

J.M. Frey

Once Upon A Time, When We Were All Bella Swan

My first crush was a sarcastic know-it-all Immortal named Methos, a character from *Highlander*. To this day I am convinced he is my perfect soulmate. And the focus of my sexual awakening. Lots of people cite The Boiler Room Scene from *My So-Called Life,* Jareth in *Labyrinth*, Colin Firth in *Pride & Prejudice,* or any/all members of the Fellowship of the Ring. But mine happened when Methos rolled out of bed in nothing but boxers to defend his life with a Roman short-sword. Unf.

When we are becoming women we all want, and we all want to be wanted, but we don't know how to go about getting it. Media texts like *Seventeen* or *Clueless,* aimed at adolescent girls, are filled with first dates, first crushes, and foot-popping first kisses. We consume them voraciously because we are desperate for any kind of clue on how this is all supposed to work. And maybe for girls who identify with these sorts of media, it's possible that it is actually helpful.

But to me as, a young goth, it wasn't. It offered me no advice and made fun of me. It labelled me a weirdo. As a baby geek, I was told that my interests and my desires weren't normal enough. Because of this, making a fool of myself in front of someone I liked was my biggest fear. My diary was filled with stories about The One picking me out of a crowd because of my Unique Specialness and sweeping me into an effortless romance where there was no fear of rejection, where he led the way so there was no fear of misstep on my part, and any fights could be resolved with passionate sex and a teary apology. I was his perfect mate in all ways.

When I reread those diaries for this piece, I was struck by how similar this narrative was to that of *Twilight, Sailor Moon,* and dozens of YA novels where the heroine is the love interest simply because of who she naturally is. This explains a lot about the popularity of these stories. These authors have tapped into that first yearning that we, as young, inexperienced but romance-hungry women, possess.

This is where fanfiction comes in, because...

Fanfiction Taught Me Everything
There Is To Know About Relationships

What is better than having the perfect romantic fantasy about a fictional character? Sharing it with your friends, of course. This isn't a new phenomenon. For as long as there has been fiction and celebrity, there have been fangirls talking about how dreamy Romeo is, or how fun Genji would be at a party, or the jerk-with-a-heart-of-gold Mr. Darcy. The Bronte Sisters had such lady-boners for the Duke of Wellington that they wrote hundreds of pages of fanfiction about the guy.

This is a natural and normal part of coming to grips with one's own blossoming libido, and the great thing about the Internet is that there's space to actually share these fantasies.

Some of them starring you.

A Mary Sue is a self-based character who is too perfect. This fanfiction trope is named for the protagonist Ensign Mary Sue from *A Trekkie's Tale* by Paula Smith, which first appeared in 1973 in a fic that lovingly lampooned them.

My first Mary Sue nobly sacrificed herself to the villain to save the series' protagonists. The villain was impressed with her bravery and instead of killing her, romances her. She redeems his soul, and they live happily ever after. It was through writing and posting these Mary Sue stories that I began to read more fanfiction.

In general, these stories are filled with the scenes that are missing, what happens after the canon story is over or with the moments that are referred to but never shown.

Many of these fics, especially the kind that deal with resolving the protagonist's sexual tension or relationships, taught me what it means to be a girlfriend, wife, or lover. Here were stories written by women of every age, from every walk of life, and they weren't just writing about first kisses and Mary Sues. They were writing about domestic situations, about buying curtains, about fighting over the remote, about miscarriages and bringing home baby, about wedding nights and divorces.

These female writers were filling the worlds of fiction that I loved so much with a sort of realism that was absent in other media. They were telling stories based on their own lived experiences, even if they were happening in fantastical worlds.

Here, finally, was a roadmap to my kind of romance.

And more than that...

Fanfiction Taught Me Everything
I Know About The Mechanics of Sex

The first time I felt my nipples get hard, I was reading fanfiction. I had read about nipples getting hard, but I'd never felt it before. It was weird, and warm, and sort of scratchy. It made the rest of my boob feel like it was anticipating something. Never before had my body done something like this without my say-so. It was strange. It was neat. It was a little bit scary. But fanfiction had already normalized it for me, so I wasn't freaked out.

The first time I got wet, I didn't know what it was. I was having a vivid fantasy about a boy in my class. I thought that my period had come without me knowing. Only when I went to the bathroom to check, it wasn't red.

I'd been reading a lot of male slash then (slash = romances between two same gendered characters, who usually in the original fiction are straight), so I didn't know that girls got wet. It never occurred to me to ask my mother what it was, and Google and many of the sex-and-body-positive sites didn't exist as a resource yet. Then I realized that it was slippery like the lube that the male characters used in anal sex in fanfiction.

"Cool!" I thought. "Girls make their own lube! Bravo, Mother Nature!"

I later confirmed this with a quick read of the foreplay parts of some M/F fanfiction, and a look through an honest-to-god hardcopy encyclopedia.

Through fanfiction I learned about BDSM, and the tenets of "safe, sane, and consensual". I read stories featuring blood play, puppy play, sugar daddies, and professional sex workers. I read stories about tentacle sex, mind sex, and alien pollen that Makes You Do It. I read about safe sex, realistic sex, sex that was awful and aborted halfway through. I read about dental dams, condoms, and IUDs. I read about sex that was filled with laughter, and sex that gets away from you, sex that gets a little too violent and requires a conversation after, and sex that wasn't violent enough and required a frank discussion of fulfilling kinks.

My favourite was, and is, the Alpha/Beta/Omega dynamic stories, where beyond their primary biological sex (breeder, breed-ee, or neither) characters have a secondary gender which defines their place in society. These question what gender and sex really are in our world. Traits commonly assigned to each gender on the inherently flawed binary scale are blown apart, reassigned, or done away with all together. These are stories where gender fluidity, pansexuality, and trans bodies are celebrated and explored, where societies outside of a patriarchy are discussed. It questions what their pitfalls and advantages would be. And this arms readers with the vocabulary and critical thinking to take back into their real lives and start discussions.

Discussions, I realized, that I was starting to have with myself, because...

Fanfiction Taught Me Everything There Is To Know About Questioning the Default "Straight" Setting

While fanfiction was addressing the parts of the stories that we never got to see, it was *also* addressing the parts of our society and culture that are obscured, hidden, or taboo. I was a teenager in the days before same-sex marriage was legal in Canada, when there were maybe only five queer characters on television, and erotica was not the mainstream hit that it is today. The only canonical lesbian I had ever seen on TV was Ellen.

But in fanfiction anything was fair game. If we could turn

protagonists into vampires, bounty hunters, or elves, we could sure as heck turn them homosexual, bisexual, asexual, or any of the wonderful, beautiful in-betweens. Characters slid all over the rainbow. And through fanfiction I learned about identities like transgendered, genderfluid, and demisexual.

Fanfiction writers, especially queer ones, found their voices by borrowing a character's. They forced room for themselves within narratives that excluded them. They appropriated the white, the straight, the cis, the male and they transformed it into the sorts of people they were or saw around themselves. And in doing so, they made me, the white, straight, cis girl accept their voices as authentic and human.

And the more stories I read featuring a variety of arrangements of genitals and sexualities, the more I started to recognize myself in those written impulses. With the revelations they offered, the veils were pulled back.

I realized I wasn't as straight as I thought I was.

At this point, I'd had a number of very intimate friendships with girls. The kind where we shared a bed and giggled together until dawn, we gave each other massages, went skinny dipping. We told each other stories where we were the girlfriends of our favourite boy band members and told each other our first confusing, awkward, tingly-making sex dreams.

But those girls all wanted to kiss boys. And I sort of...wanted to kiss them. Which was weird, right? All those mainstream media texts told me that I was supposed to want to kiss boys, too.

So I started researching the right label for what I was.

While I was touring university campuses, I screwed up my courage and told my parents I was bisexual. It was the label that made the most sense to me at the time.

I liked fantasizing about Methos. But I liked Xena, too.

"How can you know that?" my mother asked. "You've never even kissed a girl."

I hadn't kissed a boy then yet, either. Yet it was assumed that I was straight because that was the default, even though I hadn't done anything with anyone.

That shocked me.

For the first time I really understood that people were assumed straight until proven otherwise. That people around me thought that the world really was like it was portrayed on television, and not at all as diverse and colourful as I had read about in fanfiction.

I feared that Mom was right. I had internalized my own assumed default straightness to such an extent that I felt like a fraud calling myself bisexual.

And then in my first year of university I met Her.

We were best friends. I wanted desperately to be more. But I was so shy, too inexperienced, and in the end too naive to ask for it. For all I learned about sex and romance from fanfiction, nothing I had read so far had taught me how to say "I want you in ways I didn't think I could, and it scares the ever-loving frack out of me." I wished I could put on *Xena* and turn to her and say, "You know, I feel the same way about you that Gabrielle feels for Xena."

But she didn't use fandom as a cipher to convey meaning the way I had learned to do. In the end, our friendship crumbled. In part, I think, because of all the things we couldn't say or allow ourselves to be to one another. It was ugly. She had been my everything for four years.

I moved to Japan to get my head on straight. There was one boy there, and I dated him with relish, embracing my Bi-ness. He was a geek and an astrophysicist to boot which was, unf, the sexiest thing on the planet. "Tell me again about how string theory works?" I would ask over dinner and fail to catch everything because I couldn't stop looking at his mouth. He taught me that "PhD" were the three sexiest letters in the English language, and that I fell for brains and needed to adore someone intellectually, before any sexual feelings could develop. He was called up to NASA and that ended that.

Coming back to Canada, I met another amazing Her, and when she had broken my heart by laughing off my every advance as The Cute Bisexual Is Experimenting, I met the He that I was certain I would marry. He was very certain that we wouldn't.

Being bisexual isn't easy. Some lesbians don't want to be with a woman who has ever touched a dick. Some straight guys think sleeping with other women is just to get their attention. Lots of people tell me that I need to pick a side, already.

But these frustrations were never unexplainable to me, because...

Fanfiction Taught Me Everything
There Is To Know About Starting Discussions

I had some sexual escapades. Some were with women. Some were with men. Mostly they were unsatisfying, not because my lovers were inexperienced or bad, but because there was still something *missing*.

It's not like I couldn't get my own motor running; I wrote pretty racy sex scenes back when I wrote fanfiction and I did my best to give my readers the same sorts of stories, tools, and discussions that those fanfiction writers gave me when I was reading their erotica.

The question was: if it wasn't the sex, then what was wrong?

Labels are useful. Some people don't like them – they say they shut people up in impenetrable boxes, don't allow for variances, or play into the narcissistic desire of the Millennial Generation to define themselves in ways that make them special, special snowflakes. I've heard every argument there is against labels.

But I think they are good starting points. They are words that can be used to get everyone on the same page and at the same point; how it diverges from there is a matter of the discussion, and how the person using the label explains themselves. And how labels can change over time, and that's okay, too.

Through fanfiction I discovered asexual!Sherlock and greyace!Spock, bisexual!Steve Rogers, demisexual!Rodney McKay, homoromantic!Xena. And of course, my beloved Methos, having lived through five thousand years of sociocultural sexual norms that change with each new empire he watched rise and crumble. My Methos, whose sexuality flowed like a river, filling the shape of whatever vessel he chose as his secret identity that decade.

So here's my label: Demisexual biromantic greyace.

For those not in the know, a demisexual is someone who only (or mostly) experiences sexual desire to someone with whom they hold a deep intellectual and emotional attachment, and is in reference to the physical side of attraction. A biromantic is someone who usually experiences and engages in romantic attraction and relationships with both men and women (cis or trans), and deals with the emotional side of attraction. And a greyace is an individual who does not normally experience sexual attraction, but may experience it under rare or specific circumstances. Alternately, a greyace may feel sexual attraction, but have no desire to act on it, like crushing on a hot actor.

It seems like a mouthful but it's a starting point. It's a definition to point to and say: "This is what I am. Can you be with me if these are the limitations? Great, now let's talk about the places where these labels are permeable."

Because of fanfiction, I know who I am. Fanfiction has armed me with the knowledge, the confidence, and the vocabulary to talk about who I am, and what I want.

Where, like Methos', my sexuality finally flows.

A Divorcee's Guide to the Apocalypse

Katie West, illustration by Kristen Gudsnuk

How do you survive the end of love?
Same way you survive the end of the world.

I'm a divorcee. But I'm not sad, angry, or broken, and neither is my former husband. When I tell people I'm recently divorced, the look they always give me? I know pity when I see it. I understand that reaction; marriage is this thing, this contract, this relationship that is supposed to last forever. The entire goal of marriage is to have no end, 'til death do us part and whatever. When I tell people that my marriage has ended, the only seemingly appropriate reaction is to mourn the broken promises and then politely inquire as to my well-being. This is a reaction I don't appreciate because it takes away from the work I have done to survive the end of love.

Think about it this way, if you'd seriously and diligently prepared for the apocalypse so that, when it finally happened, not only did you survive, but you thrived, would you like people to treat you delicately and with sympathy? I want people to high-five me and congratulate me on discovering a new way of living, to celebrate with me my new understanding: that survival is insufficient.

I understand that my circumstances may be unique, but I also think it's important to know that we don't have to go through particular life events the same way as everyone else or feel the way that others expect us to. I believe that Apocalyptic survival – both literal and matrimonial – is best achieved in two phases: Phase 1 is Survival. If you make it through this, you can move on to Phase 2: Knowing that Survival is Insufficient. This phrase comes from an episode of *Star Trek: Voyager* (my favourite Trek) and is used to express the importance of freedom and individual choice. It's used to recognize the difference between surviving and living. I'm sharing this with you because the apocalypse of my marriage was one of the best things that ever happened to me, and I'm going to tell you why, and how.

Phase 1: Survival

Everyone preparing for the apocalypse should understand the basic Rule of Three if they hope to be successful: three weeks without food kills you, three days without water kills you, and three hours without shelter kills you. These rules can handily be applied to marriage, too.

So when the world ends, what will you do? Have you thought about it much? I have. I've thought about it a lot and the first thing I'm going to do when shit goes south is find my former husband, Matt. We've talked about the apocalypse and how it will happen and our plans to survive. We've discussed infectious diseases, economic collapse, famine, flooding, environmental disasters, and nuclear war. We have an outcome for every eventuality; chance of survival is always slim – we're realists – but if we make it, we have plans. We voraciously read post-apocalyptic books and watched post-apocalyptic movies. We planned our escape routes and discussed weapons of choice. But while we were busy planning for the apocalypse, our marriage ended.

If the end of my marriage was like any particular kind of apocalyptic event, it would have been a slow flood. You know it's raining – raining quite a bit actually – and you keep waiting for it to stop, but eventually you accept it's not going to. That this is it. As we noticed the world was starting to flood, we were angry and blamed each other, but when the end of the world comes, there's always more than one person to blame, so you've just got to get out a lifejacket, pack up your gear, and go searching for a boat. The thing that most people don't understand though, is that while it was raining, my husband held the umbrella for me so I could put on my lifejacket, and while he searched for a boat,

I kept his gear dry. By the time the flood waters were at our knees we knew that there could be life after this, but we'd have to take separate boats. We spent the last few months of our marriage just preparing to set out alone.

The end came five years and three months after we said our vows and, because of our preparation, very little changed when it did. In essence, the apocalypse of our love had come, but we had food to keep us full and satiated, water to keep us hydrated and clear, and shelter to keep us safe and warm.

Phase 1a: Food

When you're not hungry you feel one of two ways: either you don't even notice it, or you feel very comfortable, safe, and content. To feel that way in my marriage meant I needed money, as unromantic as that sounds. Not having the money to buy the things you need is extremely stressful and gives a marriage a very anxious undertone. There have been long periods of time in my life, and in my marriage, where I had no money and had to rely on the kindness of strangers to support me and, by extension, my husband. This is probably why, even though I am a picky eater, I will eat any food as long as it is free; so here's hoping that with whatever apocalyptic event we're faced also comes the demise of capitalism and the destruction of our current monetary structures.

And speaking of free: do you know what's free in a world where the apocalypse hasn't happened yet? That's right, basically nothing. But being married makes much easier living life in a world where nothing is free, which, in turn, can make separating a lot more difficult. Maybe alone you can make twenty bucks last for three weeks, but married life means you have forty bucks. Married life means two people sharing all the bills *and* you get a bigger apartment, a faster Internet connection, and you eat more than just Kraft Dinner and pizza, theoretically. So, if you're the person in the relationship who makes less money, separating from your partner often means separating from the quality of life you've become used to. Your life suddenly becomes stretched, spread over distances you didn't even know existed, let alone how to navigate on your own.

But if you're the person who makes more money – say almost twice as much as your partner – then you're me, and you feel like you're creating a situation where your partner will starve. If food is required for survival, and money is food, then the best way I could ensure both Matt's and my own survival was to share what I had. Which is why we lived together for eight months after we separated, shared a credit card for over a year, and just split our Netflix account a week ago. Neither of us starved, both of us stayed comfortable, safe, and content. This is probably not a very popular piece of advice, but if you're aiming for mutually assured survival after divorce, sometimes that means sharing your food stores with someone who no longer shares your table.

Phase 1b: Water

Finding fresh water during an apocalyptic event is paramount. Three days! You only have three days to come across a water source that isn't contaminated, stagnant, or, you know, an ocean. Three days is also about as long as I could go without talking to my husband; my need to communicate was a thirst, especially as things got more difficult. It is the very nature of language to flow, and so, like water during end times, words during a marriage are paramount. Finding the right ones, those without salt, without toxicity, is a skill that helped me survive my divorce. My former husband is my best friend. I say 'former' because 'ex' sounds so shallow, so rough. The language we use to talk of the end of things is often small and sharp, like the wreckage of ships jutting up from a calm sea. Look at the 'end' compared to the 'beginning'; everyone is so verbose at the beginning of things.

The language my former husband and I used at the beginning of our marriage was not in keeping with this idea. Our words have always been small, but instead of sharp, they've been full, they've quenched in single gulps. We lived our entire marriage knowing there would be an end. In our minds, it was the end of the world, not the end of the marriage, but it still resulted in an urgency to get to exactly how we were feeling. The end of the world doesn't have time for you to sit around and think about what you want to say; the apocalypse demands you say it now, say what you mean, choose your words with conviction, this may be your last chance. So that's how we spent our marriage, saying what we meant and waiting for the end that would make it all justified. We were great communicators. These words kept us sated, so we continue to share them. Our words to one another are a bracing fresh water source we can draw from anytime we get thirsty out here beyond the end of marriage.

Phase 1c: Shelter

In some apocalyptic circumstances, finding shelter will be no problem. If, for example, a virus wipes out 99 percent of the planet's population, there's going to be a lot of empty houses. However, if we find ourselves in a nuclear wasteland or a *Waterworld* situation, shelter may be more difficult to come by. In marriage, think of love as your shelter. Love can be something you stumble upon when you weren't really looking, or it can be hard to come by no matter how badly you need it. But the fact remains, you can only survive three hours without shelter in harsh environments, and divorce can be a very harsh environment. Many people get divorced because they're no longer in love with the person they married, and that's okay; there is more love being put out into the world than there are people to receive it and they will find love again. But at the end of my marriage, my love didn't end.

I loved my husband from the day he emailed me in university and all it said was, "What's your story, Katie West?" The first time we hung out, we were both seeing other people, and we sat in the basement of the university library and he told me his theories on the end of the world. And I told him mine. And that day we started making plans, not about the future of us, but for what we would do in a future so doomed to fail. I loved him not like in teen vampire movies and epic fantasy books; it wasn't romantic – it was necessary. I needed a place to keep my heart safe and Matt was it. He became the walls that protected me from harsh winds of criticism, the roof that kept me dry when my depression stormed around me, he generated the heat that kept me stable and functioning. And when we built this shelter, we built it strong enough to weather a flood, so it remains to this day. The love I felt hasn't really changed; it has remained as four sturdy walls and a roof over my head. People think this is weird, if I still love my husband, why did we get divorced? Because survival is insufficient. Even during the apocalypse, you eventually have to leave the shelter and start to live again.

Phase 2: Survival is Insufficient

The phrase 'Survival is Insufficient' highlights the difference between surviving and actually living. This is Phase 2 of the

Apocalyptic Survival Plan, wherein surviving is not enough. Survive and you're Max instead of Furiosa; survive and you're Katniss instead of Peeta; survive and you're Sergeant Ed Parks instead of Melanie. You might think you're fine, and people may even see you as the hero of the story because you *survived*; you survived the end of love and what could be more difficult than that?

What's more difficult is what comes after. When it's done, when the smoke clears and you receive your official divorce papers in the mail, you ask yourself now who are you – *what* are you? This is when you realize survival is insufficient. Just getting through it with food, water, and shelter isn't enough. Now you must create new habits and ways of being, ones that push you forward towards a life that is scary and fills you with anxiety and is most definitely the best life you've ever had. A new habit can be as seemingly insignificant as sleeping in the middle of the bed, to something more substantial like taking up new hobbies. I did weird things, like shoemaking, tried watercolour painting, refreshed my high school skills with sewing classes, and pushed my body into new positions with yoga. I did all of these new things by myself. I wanted to understand, after over five years of marriage, who I was when I was alone.

While I was married, I was surviving a slow flood; after I was divorced, I was living a life I chose. I quit my job. I switched careers. I moved to a new continent. I wasn't running away – I was choosing to live. I do a lot of things now that I didn't do before; small things like drink cocktails and meet more than one person at a time, but also big things like write seriously and see a vague outline of forever.

Don't fear the end. The apocalypse can be a herald of death and loneliness, just as divorce can be a herald of loss and loneliness, but though these endings are scary times, you can survive, and you can thrive. The end of the world is coming, but I came out of a marriage happy and free and with a friend who will always have my back, so the apocalypse can suck it.

Cherry

*Cherelle Higgins with illustrations by Rachael Wells,
and colour by Meaghan Carter*

My first love was a cyborg.

Steve Austin, astronaut. A man barely alive. They rebuilt him.
Better than he was before. Better...stronger...faster.

But he was American. I was English. He was fictional, I was seven.

It was doomed from the start.

I was resilient, I moved on. Clark Kent, then David Banner – whom
I later came to know as "Bruce," Doc Savage, Green Lantern...my
favourites were all tall, muscular, and mysterious.

Until Frodo Baggins. I adored Frodo. I chose well; Frodo saved my
life.

I first read *Lord of the Rings* when I was eight. I signed it out of the
school library in September and every two weeks for years. It was
intricate and wordy, a struggle, but worth it every time. Middle Earth
was nothing if not orderly and fair, and I craved that.

Before I started secondary school, I had to return the copy to the
primary school library. That summer I saved my pocket money and
bought my own.

It was dog-eared before the new school year started.

This was the fall of 1981, in a small country town just outside of
Watford, Hertfordshire. England.

Thatcher's England, at the height of unemployment and in the
throes of a race war. The Brixton riots had just happened and we felt

its impact. National Front graffiti suddenly covered every flat surface and I learned to associate a swastika with terror long before I learned what a concentration camp was.

Up until that point, casual racism had been an everyday fact of life for me. It wasn't really even offensive, merely expected. It was the substrate on which all my experiences were built.

But now, "preference" and "bias" had given way to hate. Hate aimed at people like my Jamaican family, and mixed people like me, their adopted daughter – a brown-skinned frizzy-haired mongrel child.

I was blissfully oblivious to most of this, being bookish and 11 years old. On the first day of school, as I dressed in my new uniform, I had no idea what was waiting for me, and would be waiting for me every weekday afternoon for the next several months.

I loved my school uniforms. Each morning was a comforting ritual of buttons, hooks and zippers. I would clean my pink NHS spectacles, then my mother would braid my hair into a tight, frayed rope and slick down the errant fluff with Vaseline.

I was freaking magnificent.

The first day of school was uneventful.

Between classes and at lunch, I was blissfully invisible, enveloped by a sea of navy blue, with a thousand other girls dressed identically. They were not a family, less than a tribe, but I belonged there...my clothing was proof.

Then the train ride home.

That first day, I got off the train and headed down the ramp to the foot tunnel at the bottom, bustling South Oxhey to the left, my sleepy town to the right. Most of the crowd went left, leaving me exposed.

Leaning on the wall ahead of me was a tall skinny punk, hair high in a green mohawk, all black leather and metal – and boots that I would later get to know quite intimately.

Slightly hunched, and sneering over his cigarette he looked, for all the world, like an orc. The largest pin on his jacket read "Enoch was Right".

"Enoch the Orc" I thought. I smiled and kept walking.

Suddenly, "Oi!! What you smiling at, Paki?" I kept walking, no longer smiling.

The next day there were four of them.

From then on, my days were slashed in two; the time before The Beating, and the time after.

The event itself was an exercise in reflex and detached observation.

Boots were the weapon of choice, so they became my specialty. Doctor Martens were softer soled, round toed, the diffuse impact lacked the bite of the army boot and the electrifying precision of the metal tipped motorcycle boot favoured by Enoch himself.

Doctor Martens were preferred.

I had no interest in their names, only their styles. Who was a Kicker, who was a Stomper, who would hang back to take the finishing blow for himself.

They were consistent.

After that first week, I learned to adjust. I tried arriving later, dawdled on the platform, or rode the train to the magically named Hatch End station to buy myself more time, in the hopes that they would find a distraction.

But they were always there. They had nothing else to do.

My skin made me a target; their boredom made me their project.

I learned the art of fixing scuffed patent leather shoes with a black crayon and how to become presentable before my parents got home. My mother complimented me on my sudden interest in hygiene as my uniform was always washed and hung to dry without instruction or cajoling.

It never once occurred to me to tell my parents. The bruises were covered by my clothing, and my mother's penchant for "traditional" discipline had left me well equipped to handle physical discomfort.

Early the following spring, after a short but painful winter, The Boy appeared.

One Saturday, while perched on the deep ledge of my bedroom window, I glanced up from my book and there he was – working in the garden with my father. He was scrawny, in that new-growth way of teenage boys; all legs and with a crest of gloriously feathered hair. He looked up and waved.

Despite my sincere belief that any interactions with boys would render me immediately and shamefully pregnant, I waved back.

These days the sudden appearance of a helpful, pretty white boy in a front yard might not be cause for alarm, but for my parents it was both flattering and troubling.

My mother would search my face for a glimmer of interest every time the subject came up. I feigned stoic boredom, but listened carefully over the sound of my pounding heart, waiting for his name. It was never mentioned.

And every Saturday I would sit hopefully in my front window. The Boy would wave, I would wave back, my ears would burn. Once I ventured outside while they were working, ostensibly to offer "help". I lasted only a few minutes. I returned to my window perch, flustered and breathless. But I had been close enough to learn a vital new piece of information: his eyes were hazel.

Now Frodo, fragile, brave and loyal, had The Boy's face. On days when I was feeling particularly adventurous, Sam had mine.

The month before the end of the school year, The Boy stopped coming.

Life went on.

The after-school shenanigans were sporadic now, the Orcs had lost their leader around Valentine's Day and they had neither the leadership or organizational skills for a sustained attack, so for a short while, I was allowed to pass with a bit of shoving and name calling.

Some days they weren't there at all.

I had even stopped wearing my winter coat. The weather was warmer, but more importantly, my adversaries were bored and half-hearted in their attacks. Enoch was gone and Army Boots had none of the discipline his footwear might have suggested, so I thought I no longer needed the extra armour.

I was wrong.

The last time I saw the Orcs, they were waiting at the bottom of the ramp, as usual. I didn't look up as I passed them, and I felt them fall into their usual step behind me...waiting for me to cross that magical borderline between government property and the town itself.

"So this is what you lot do with your time then, eh?"

An adult male voice.

For a moment I was relieved.

Then I saw them on the embankment above the path.

Skinheads.

They jumped down and blocked my way.

Until that moment, I had thought of the boys who harassed me as "men". They were not. They were only recently children themselves, and deep inside I knew they would never really try to break me. My refusal to cry had earned me a grudging respect, and besides, I was their only toy.

They had never even drawn blood.

If they were Orcs, then standing before me now was an Uruk-hai, bald, ugly, scarred; his eyes bright with something I would not be able to name until I was much older.

Behind him, I saw a face I had often dreamed about.

The Boy. His head shaved like the rest of them, cherry red Doctor Martens brand new, unscuffed.

His eyes never met mine.

That night, I hid from my parents.

Years later while sitting in a doctor's office, I would be asked "have you ever cracked a rib?" then suddenly I had a name for the gasping pain all those years before.

Early the following morning, there was a gentle knock on our front door.

My father answered.

I never saw who my father spoke to, but when I left for school, my book was sitting on our garden wall. I had watched it being torn apart, but here it was, the spine clumsily taped together.

I left it there.

That afternoon, and every afternoon until we left for Canada, my father picked me up from school.

I never saw The Boy again and it would be almost exactly 20 years before I would let myself revisit Middle Earth.

In the decades of my self-imposed exile I moved on. I found Clarke, Bradbury, Herbert and Asimov and embraced their muddy, human morality. I found my own tribe, or they found me, and the Orcs faded into metaphor.

The Boy remained; sweet, sad and as trapped by circumstances as I was.

The night that I saw *The Fellowship of the Ring* for the first time, my roommate found me standing unsteadily in the front hallway of our house. Later he said he thought someone had died.

"Are you okay?"

I nodded, unable to find words.

"It sucked?"

I shook my head violently.

"It was...perfect," I croaked.

Well, almost perfect.

In College (1971) I STILL drew stories and found out other people DID want to read stuff.... SORT OF like mine!

Hey, I bet I could do a story WAY better than THIS!

Discovered in 1973!

WIMMENS COMIX

I continued writing the stories that I wanted to read. Since nobody ELSE was.

And, OTHER people get to read it! FAR OUT!

mmm..

My SECOND submission to Wimmens Comix got rejected, so I decided to print my own darn comic book! (So, THERE!)

Hey- nobody's gonna tell ME my comics won't get published...

Fortunately, I got lots of help. Joyce Farmer, Lyn Chevli, Phil Yeh. --and as usual, some weirdness...

Dynamite Damsels! GREAT title!

The OWNER saw your... uh-- COMIC... We can finish up this ONE job for you but after THAT...

The printer

I could also do stories for "Tits & Clits" and later, "Gay Comix".. -- whenever "real Life" wasn't getting in the way.

We TOLD YOU she was BAD NEWS...

He's LYING! You'll be DITCHED in a few weeks..

-- But you'll always have -- US!

A..Transexual guy.. what if he.. or she... had a former life.. and then comes BACK?

A story about an abusive lesbian alcoholic? I just ESCAPED from one..

This..person comes from some-- OTHER place --and cant believe how obsessed humans are with.. who's "WHO"!

I finally said to HELL with "love" and came home at night (after tedious day jobs) to my ever-faithful MUSES!

Wow, this is the coolest thing ever! And I'm doing it!

It's a COMIC, so you have to read the dialogue, and you can't hear what sort of voice the person has...

- AND, no PRONOUNS!

I'd fuss with the art into the wee hours, then sleep with the big portfolio comfortingly close by.

Eventually, I published the first half of the appropriately-titled "Winging It" as a "graphic novel."

YOU PAID GOOD MONEY TO PRINT.. THIS TRASH?

Family

Don't listen to them..

"A waste of the air and water that made the trees that made the paper it was printed on.."

"Review"

TO WHO?

In the pre-digital 1980s, the books trickled into the hands of a few VERY appreciative readers who just LOVED it and sent me some long letters and wonderful gifts.

Books! Artwork- MUSIC! I gotta get the REST of "Winging it" done..

But in 1989 I made a BIG move before finishing the second half of it ....

Gee, Fantagraphics wants to publish a COMIC of mine!

Nothing more inspiring than putting together a lot of OTHER folks' comics!

Anybody remember DARKROOMS?

80

Both Sides of the Table and Between the Sheets

Janet Hetherington, and an interview with Jackie Estrada

"At last, my heart's an open door, and
My secret love's no secret anymore."
– Doris Day, singing as Calamity Jane

It's difficult these days to imagine a time without comic-cons. Today's glitzy, media-focused events are plastered all over television and the Internet, and you can go to them almost at any time, all over the world.

And fans do. Over 130,000 fans of all stripes flocked to Comic-Con International (CCI) in San Diego, California – long considered the mother of all comic-cons – in 2015.

For a geek girl with a secret love of comic books, it's nerdvana.

To understand the import of this cultural shift, we must hop into the TARDIS (or Bill and Ted's most excellent phone booth, or Doc Brown's DeLorean, or a Hot Tub Time Machine) and travel back to a time when comic-cons were far and few between.

First time point touch-down:
Late 1960s, small-town Ontario, Canada

When I was growing up, liking comic books was a guy thing. I

guess I didn't know any better, because I read comic books – a lot of comic books – but I was often embarrassed by them. I devoured DC Comics' romance titles (*Young Romance, Falling in Love, Secret Hearts*), but when I made my Wednesday run to the convenience store, I would take the romance comic books and hide them underneath the *Superman, Batman, Lois Lane, Wonder Woman, Green Lantern* and *Flash* comics when I was paying at the register. As if the man at the counter cared!

But I loved reading those comic books, and in that pre-Twitter era, I expressed my love by writing letters to the publisher. I sent poems and drawings, and some even got published.

Did I think for one moment that I could make a career for myself writing and drawing comics? No. In my mind, that too was a guy thing.

I did, however, know that *Daily Planet* reporter Lois Lane got paid for her writing, plus she snagged a celebrity boyfriend (Superman, no less), so I followed her path and studied journalism at Carleton University in Ottawa.

A couple of interesting things happened at Carleton. I discovered

Marvel Comics; I started writing articles about comic books for specialty publications like *Amazing Heroes*; and in 1979, I became involved with organizing a local science fiction and comic book convention called Maplecon. Comic-cons were not the norm, so if we wanted one, we had to create one.

Veer to a new time-point touch-down:
1970, San Diego, United States
Where another geek girl is already deep into making comic-con history

It may have felt like I was alone in my passion for comics and related genres, but the truth was, other girls were also breaking the mold. "I have been to every San Diego Comic-Con, starting with the first three-day event in 1970," confesses Jackie Estrada, publisher of Exhibit A Press, author of *Comic Book People 1 & 2* and former president of Friends of Lulu. "I started volunteering at the convention in 1974 or 1975. Among the many jobs I held over the first few decades were editor of Comic-Con publications, Artists' Alley coordinator, PR person, and pro registration coordinator. I became administrator of the Will Eisner Comic Industry Awards in 1990."

Fast-forward to the 1990s:
Transition from fan-girl to professional

San Diego Comic-Con continued going strong in the 1990s, but Ottawa's Maplecon held its final show in 1992. Still, something major happened in fandom…more girls and women began to embrace genre media (comics, science fiction, horror, videogames) revealing their inner fan and started attending conventions, a trend that continues today.

"We're definitely seeing more women and girls at shows," Jackie says. "I originally noticed it in the mid-1990s with the burgeoning popularity of manga and anime. Females have also gotten into comics and the popular arts via such routes as *Star Wars* fandom and cosplay. Today I see a lot more female creators and readers in the kids and YA categories, following the success of titles such as Raina Telgemeier's *Smile* and *Drama*."

Indeed, the 1990s saw a rise in female convention attendees and in female creators. These ladies weren't necessarily doing mainstream superhero comic books. They were inspired to follow their own vision and tell their own stories. In her 1999 book *From Girls to Girrrlz: A History of Women's Comics from Teens to Zines*, author and comic book creator Trina Robbins offers an explanation for the shift. "Many of the young women, many in their tweens and twenties, had been brought up in non-sexist and non-traditional ways by mothers who themselves had been part of the 'second wave feminism' of the 1970s," she wrote.

While Trina goes on to talk about young women creating "grrrl" comics – no longer well-mannered, pink-ribboned 'nice girls,' as she puts it – I believe these creators, often starting out as fans, were saying "I can do that" and giving themselves permission to actively play in the sandbox with the guys.

That includes slipping between the sheets.

The ladies of the 1990s were no longer waiting at home by the telephone for Mr. Right, as Roy Lichtenstein so artfully immortalized.

Mr. Right was at the comic-con, so the ladies set forth. Today, geek speed dating and social mixers are commonplace at comic book conventions.

When asked if comic-cons are a good place for people to meet and fall in love, Jackie says, "Well, it worked for me! I can't really speak for anyone else, but if you are pursuing something you love and you run into other people who love the same thing, you just might find your soul mate."

Jackie met her husband, artist Batton Lash (creator of *Wolff & Byrd, Counselors of the Macabre*) in 1990 at the Chicago ComiCon over the Fourth of July weekend.

"I was travelling with Fae Desmond, Comic-Con's Executive Director," Jackie says. "We met Batton and his friend Russell Calabrese at DC's party, and Bat and I hit it off pretty quickly. At the San Diego Comic-Con three weeks later, I had a get-together at my house for people who were in town early for the show, as well as Comic-Con staffers and made sure to include Batton and Russell. I showed Batton my original art for a complete Steve Ditko story from *Journey into Mystery*, and that pretty much sealed the deal. He moved to San Diego in the fall of 1993 and we were married in January 1994. We started Exhibit A Press to publish his comics, and the first issue of *Wolff & Byrd, Counselors of the Macabre* came out in May. He wrote and drew the book, and I was the editor and letterer. We've been publishing his work ever since, although the title has changed to *Supernatural Law*. We have a booth every year at Comic-Con and travel to other shows as well."

Back in Canada, it was a roundabout journey to meeting my own Mr. Right.

As a writer for *Amazing Heroes*, I was assigned the Canadian beat, which meant I interviewed Canadian comic creators to find out about their new projects. I connected with Ronn Sutton, artist and creator of the *Starbikers* comic book, by telephone. Ronn was living in Toronto and working as a creative director and animator. We kept in touch and even collaborated via mail on artwork appearing in the *San Diego Comic-Con Souvenir Book*. We finally met in person at Maplecon. We both have versions of how we got together. My story is PG-13 and Ronn's story is... spicier.

Ronn moved to Ottawa in 1992, and we formed Hetherington/

Sutton Studio in 1994. One of our first collaborations was a newspaper comic strip called *Jannie Weezie*, about a comic book writer and artist living together. Ronn pursued comic book work, but we got a chance to collaborate on a number of other projects, including the *Spinnerette* horror series for Millennium Comics. I began joining Ronn behind the table as a professional comics creator for the first time.

Remember those romance comic books I was embarrassed to read when I was a kid? Those comics haunted me, and then inspired me. I wrote, drew and self-published my own comic book series, *Eternal Romance*, in 1997. That same year, I was asked by Jackie to be a judge for the 1997 Eisner Awards.

Time jump to the 2000s:
Firmly positioned behind the table

Other opportunities arose. Ronn began drawing *Elvira, Mistress of the Dark* for Claypool Comics and I began scripting stories for *Elvira,* among other comic book projects. I also continued my Lois

Lane impression – writing for *Animation* magazine, Animation World Network, and becoming Managing Editor of WizardWorld.com for a brief period.

Sling-shot around the sun:
Back to 2015

Today, attendance at comic-cons continues to skyrocket as superhero movies and comics-inspired TV shows spawn a whole new generation of fans. Parents bring their babies to conventions, dressed as little Bat-mites and Wonder babies. Where I live, Ottawa Comiccon is held on Mother's Day weekend. No problem. Mom wants to be at the show.

Comics continue to consume my life and have certainly taken over my house. Ronn and I regularly attend comic-cons across Canada and elsewhere. My geek love is no secret anymore, and the same holds true for Jackie.

"I've been reading science fiction, fantasy, horror, and mystery books since childhood, and I've read comics since the 1950s," Jackie says. "I joined comics fandom in the mid-1960s and was a subscriber to every fanzine out there at the time. Like I said, I've been to every San Diego Comic Con. So I guess that would qualify me as a 'geek girl.' None of my loves are secret – they are all out there for the world to see."

Amen, sister.

Fanfiction, F/F, Angst

Tini Howard

In fanfiction, there's something called *the pronoun problem*. When writing a same sex couple, it can be difficult to distinguish who is who, when writing in the third person. It's not as easy as *his* and *hers*, as *she* and *he*. He kisses him, and she arches under her touch.

We get clunky, when we write fanfiction, to write around those problems. The blonde kisses the brunette. The short one begs the tall one for more. Sometimes we use occupations – the pilot nibbles the captain's ear. The warrior shudders as the witch bites her skin.

We were both writers, her and I, so that didn't work for us.

I don't remember how we met, so that story isn't part of our canon. We met in school, because we were young. We became friends. We played videogames, and watched movies over and over, clutching ourselves at subtext and glances. We gifted each other dozens of stories that never really happened, fictions of fictions.

I remember her here, first – my father had moved back in after my parents' separation. It was Sunday, and I was waiting for her to come pick me up. We had important plans to spend the last few hours of our weekend at a flea market, looking for old books and ugly clothes. Before I left, my parents called me into the other room.

"Your dad's moving out again." Clouds moved over the sun and the whole room felt cold.

"Okay," I said. "Stop bothering me with this stuff," I said. The phone rang, and I went outside. She asked me what was up and I shrugged it off.

We liked angst, it made for great stories, but real world pain was too exhausting, a distraction from our heady fantasies.

In fanfiction there's a lot of *angst*. Where everywhere else in the world, *angst* is a bad thing, something we pick on, to us it was sacred. From the well of angst and the sharp red pangs of despair came the brain-melting impulses that made fanfiction great. Nothing convinces a character to make a bad decision like the white-hot needle of pain.

Pain was beautiful. It made our stories, so deviant from the established canon, possible.

I don't know why we always wrote about boys kissing boys. At the time it was just a fetish for two very strange girls. Like so many of our pubescent sisters, we ached to be the Daphne for some young Apollo, but all that sunlight seemed stressful. We wore big black sweaters and boots that were our Christmas-and-birthday presents, and our makeup wasn't finely applied or made to withstand the hot lights of the stage. We wanted to see the burning gaze of young males, but we couldn't stand to be underneath it.

I don't remember how we decided that two young boys loving each other would be the *best thing ever*, but we did. We weren't the first, and we were far from the last.

Forbidden lust, unbidden from the expectations of young women, and freed of poisoned ideas about masculinity, I could write for days about what makes slash fanfiction so appealing to young women. What I can tell you is this – if our heroes were getting dirty when we turned the TV off, it was probably okay for us to do it, too.

People who write fanfiction talk about something called *slash baiting*. It's the idea that creators know their media will be appealing to the fandom community, and they lean into that by teasing without intent. It's wrong for actual, political, LGBT reasons, but at the time, it was flaky and sweet, and we were hungry little fish.

What it really means is there's a lot of gay affection without the promise of resolution.

One of the many problems with slash baiting is that it's often realistic.

I don't remember how she talked me into it, but we spent a lot of time cuddling. I wouldn't be entirely lying if I didn't say at least part of it was mimicry, a natural urge to be like the forbidden love we adored. But there was plenty of tension, layered thick as buttercream by slumber parties where we shared beds, and she convinced, coerced with her stubby nails trailing tracks along the place where my pants and shirt never seemed to meet. We contented ourselves like cats with petting, gentle scratches, purring and shivers, the things normal girls might like. But we weren't cats. Or normal.

When I say I let her talk me into it, there's no anger there, no advantage taken. She was a hand leading me out of a cave. I was, and am, a girl for whom theory is always different from practice, a girl born in the eighties, before our parents had viral stories about talking sexuality with their kids. No one ever told me it was okay to feel this way about women, though I had my whole life, and bisexuality was nothing more than something I learned about watching Pop-Up Video. David Bowie and Mick Jagger. Secret lovers. We loved that. I was always Bowie. She was Jagger.

And we never really talked about it, anyway.

In fanfiction, I've never liked the ones with too much talking.

One of the many problems with fandom and fan works is that of explicitness. Not sex, though that's a problem too, but *explicitness*, the idea that everything must be spelled out. *The Scarlet Letter*'s "and all was spoken" is lost on much of fandom, who insists on knowing what was said, and when, who did the talking and who did the listening, and did they take turns? A scene that ends with a meaningful look between two characters and picks up again at break of day will be the source of dozens of fictions and art, endless supposition on what happened that night. These are called *missing scenes,* implying not that they are additional, but that they are essential, that like a hidden camera with a conspiracy, the lives of these characters have been edited together to show us but one side of the story.

One night, I stepped out of her closet to see if I'd look good in a borrowed dress. It was an honest question – our bodies were as different as could be, then. I was all angles and darkness, and she called me *willowy* every damn day. She was tan lines and freckles, solid muscle and short boyish hair. She was the sun, and she turned me into her tree. She was Apollo, and I was Daphne.

She pushed me into the closet and kissed me hard enough to bruise my lips. I wriggled backwards onto the shelf, wrapped my legs around her hips, because it felt good and it would have made a perfect story. Laughing, groping, it only got better. Under our combined weight of hearts and hormones the shelf snapped, sending us to the closet floor. I bruised my ass on a tennis shoe and a clog.

Her mother hollered up the stairs. We laughed ourselves sick and we lied to her – we were trying to reach something. Her mother raised an eyebrow at me on the floor, five feet ten inches of lust in her daughter's dress, and shut the door.

I would have just sighed and died to read about it.

Once we went to visit her aunt, with the promise of attending the renaissance faire the next day. We were put in the same room, same bed to sleep, a habit by adults that always left us feeling like we'd used some kind of cheat code on life.

The next day at the faire we were exhausted, but we wore dashing cloaks, she bought me a rose from a vendor, and we ruined our boots with mud.

The whole day was mutton and wet wood, flowers and fantasy, and no one looked our way once. We were ladies with our hair cut short, our eyes painted, runaways from a village and deeply in secret love.

Obviously, us lonely girls, raised on labyrinths and fairytales, who found worlds of fantasy to be secret heavens for gay heroes, well. We never wanted to leave.

I borrowed some of her mother's costume jewelry to wear with my prom dress.

I didn't go with her – I went with a boy I'd started dating.

We never had a prom night – literally or figuratively. At some point, her body wanted more, her heart wanted consummation, and I couldn't give it. Years of Catholic upbringing taught me that omission was the only acceptable sin, and by keeping our deepest, most profane desires at arm's length, we could save ourselves, somehow.

She started dating a boy I didn't like. She hopped into his car and drove off one day, the sun burning off the chrome on his spoiler. I stood there, waving, my branches in the breeze.

Years later, long after we stopped speaking, I read a comic book and it changed my life. In it, two young women fall in and out of love. The tall, dark haired one engages with a slew of awful men, all while trying to remain close friends with her best friend, a short, blonde firecracker. But they are in love, and the reader knows it. Watching the brunette deny them what she knows is there, watching the blonde turn away, time and time again, rather than stand by and watch someone hurt the woman she loves – it's painful.

Spoiler alert, as we say in fandom. It was different for them than it was for me.

Years later, I'm married to my best friend. He knows everything about me, and when I tell him I'm meeting my ex-girlfriend for coffee, he tells me to have fun.

Sitting on a bench in our pantyhose and work blouses, we peel the cardboard sleeves of our cups and laugh easily. Something grown in me stretches and smiles, my distanced love of female partnership sees our young lust for what it was, and I say something, something about her, my ex-girlfriend.

She laughs, screws her nose up like a cat, looks sixteen again. "I was wondering if that was what we were."

Yeah, I confess, that's what I'd always called us. I don't tell her how long it took me to rewrite it. I don't know her story.

I stopped reading fanfiction.

URL > IRL

Gita Jackson

I don't date as an active activity anymore. Part of that was about time – actively searching for someone to fuck and tell jokes to takes time out of my already extremely tight schedule. All the apps to shorten this process make it even worse. After I broke up with my boyfriend of two years, I'd sit in bed swiping endlessly on Tinder, realizing how little I knew about these people I was instantly rejecting.

Part of it is the strange crossroads of the things I like and who I am. Whenever I talk about my interests people are usually only into half the things I'm really about. People in the comic book store don't want to hear about artist-run galleries or basement shows. People at those basement shows politely let me run my mouth when I get on a tangent about videogames. And that's fine. That's how people are. The last guy I dated (briefly) really wanted to hear my stance on worker's rights and racism but fell asleep halfway through an episode of *Steven Universe*. In whatever relationship I get into, I have to keep some parts of myself tucked away.

Another part of it is that meeting new people is often a lesson for them on race and there is just not enough time in my life to continue delivering that lecture.

Here's the cliffnotes: I am mixed race. My mother is from India, my father is from Selma, Alabama. My features read as "black," but I am just as black as I am Indian. My parents met in California in college – you know, where people meet – and moved to New England shortly after I was born. I grew up in a mostly white suburb, on an all-white-but-us street. My brother was really into Nirvana, Nine Inch Nails, and the Smashing Pumpkins, given that he reached early adolescence in a white town in 1994, and eventually I inherited his CDs and videogames. My experience of black culture was through the things my father liked (Sly and the Family Stone, Bob Marley, Jimi Hendrix, Motown) until I started actually meeting black people in college. I was a sad teenager in the suburbs in the mid-2000s. My Chemical Romance and Bright Eyes spoke more to me, at that time, than Ankh Wearing Niggas talking about The Struggle.

My father also loved science fiction and that had a lot to do with *Star Trek*, I think. I mean, he also loved *Doctor Who* and apparently watched it on PBS, and got so excited for the new series before I had any inkling of what it was. He also loved the X-Men movies and Batman. He loves and works with computers and has been in IT for 25 years. But *Star Trek* depicted a world in which he was welcome. One that doesn't exist yet, and might never exist, but seeing this fictional universe obviously left a mark on him. Sometimes he still quotes Worf to me. Sometimes he still does a Picard impression.

We're all just products of our environments, really. It's just that my environment makes people want me to explain myself. Some of it is just curiosity, and I try to be sympathetic. I know I'm a bit peculiar, and I feel like while I relate to others well, it's hard to find people that I have an instant, strong, emotional connection with, that have the same background and experiences as me. I meet very few mixed race people, for instance. I meet very few gamers who cry in front of Rothko paintings, I meet very few artists that are obsessed with the art direction for Shin Megami Tensei.

But after a while it feels hostile. Everyone is always so fucking fascinated that I'm so unusual, so weird, so unique. First dates are less romantic and more an interrogation, with a sprinkling of feeling like an animal in the zoo. They want to know how I ended up here. They want to know who taught me. They want to know why I don't match their expectation for what my accent will sound like when I open my mouth. They want to know who gave me that Surfer Blood t-shirt (they played a show, I bought a vinyl and shirt). They want to know why my septum is pierced or why my hair is natural or if I really like the things

I like (I promise you, yes I do) or if I really finished that game (yes, I did) or if I really realized the true meaning of that anime (yes, yes, I fucking did).

Look, I just want to exist. At this moment there is nothing more attractive than someone who takes what I say about myself at face value. Someone who might only really like half the things I really like, but wants to learn about things, wants to try things they haven't tried before. And this is probably why I only flirt with people on the Internet anymore.

I met the guy I'm seeing now on the Internet. I didn't think I'd like him as much as I do, but I do. He lives in Vancouver and I live in Chicago, so it's not exactly easy. We're figuring it out. What I love about him is that he's hilarious, he's kind, he sent me a cute postcard so I'd have something with his handwriting on it, something he'd touched. And he likes me the way that I am. And he never made me explain it if I didn't want to. I don't know if that would be different if we met at a bar or at a party, but I'm not exactly interested in finding that out anymore.

Meeting people at parties is a nightmare. The music is loud, everyone is drunk, and you have to think of a reason to talk to people. There's nothing less sexy than someone screaming, "What?" into your ear. On the Internet, if someone wrote a good joke, you say so. If someone took a cute selfie, you fave it. If someone has an interesting question, you can answer it without having to talk about the weather.

My friend Kit – a coworker of my mother turned mentor/surrogate grandma – told me about the time when all her friends were into *Second Life,* before, as she said, they all discovered it wasn't actually that interesting. She met up with a few people from the game, most kind of surprised that she was usually upwards of twenty years older than them. But when they met in real life it was usually the same as speaking to each other in the game. A veil is drawn. You already know so much about that other person. Ice breakers are unnecessary. A connection has already been made – you can't fake that. When all you have for long stretches of time is talking on GChat, you end up humanizing that person more than if you bring all the baggage of meeting face to face.

Like my father, I want a world where I'm just welcome. It's hard to think that a *Star Trek* future will ever really come, but you have to hope, you know? There's no justification of why Uhura is on the bridge, she's just there. She's accepted. What is hard to find when I'm trying to meet someone the "normal" way, is that acceptance. Me and my Internet boyfriend have had a few, "Your First Black Girlfriend" moments but he looks at me like he adores me, not like he's trying to figure me out. In *Rules of Attraction*, Shannyn Sossamon's character calls it a "zhing," that sound you hear, that warmth spreading across your face when everything is just right.

When he told me that he loved me, I felt it, I heard that sound in my head. It feels weird that basic human dignity makes me love him so much.

I'm at the point where I feel like normal courtship is a human ritual that is awful from top to bottom that we've just convinced ourselves that we enjoy it. It's a hassle. It's a time suck. The highs can be high, yes, but the lows are often so very, very low. When you add any kind of modifier to your person – nerd, hipster, black, queer, female – the highs become unreachable peaks and the lows are the valleys that you live in.

When people demand that I explain myself, I don't think they care how long it took for me to understand the whole arc of my life. How long it took me to wipe off a veneer of irony when I talked about liking games or anime or KPop. How long it took me to look in the mirror and appreciate the lines of my own face, my wide nose and my big lips.

When I inevitably deliver my lecture, it's like being asked to learn to love myself all over again. It's hard to even like the people who ask me to do that. It took a lot of work to love myself. How dare you ask me to justify that?

I don't date as an active activity anymore because the work of loving myself is enough. I have long-distance relationships and crushes I'll never act on because the feeling of liking someone and being liked back is enough. I am enough. I don't want to have to explain that again.

My life is in a state of unbalance and I'm learning how to roll with it. I don't know if I'm going to have a "normal" relationship, if me and my boyfriend will live with each other, if I can even ask him to leave his country for me. But I'm okay with not knowing that, at the moment. There's something there – I finally feel it. Zhing.

SHIPPING
By Jenn Woodall

Growing up, I was always a huge nerd for the things I liked. One of my most intense obsessions was Final Fantasy 7.

I remember seeing the commercials for the game on TV as a kid...

And quickly deciding that I desperately needed that game.

GAAAASP!!

I begged and begged my parents for it along with a Playstation 1.

MOOOOMMM!! PLEEEAAAASE!!

MOOOMM MOM MOM !!!

FINAL FANTASY VII
NOW AVAILABLE
PS1   PS1

LASANGA?

PLEASE PLEASE PLEASE!!

And on Christmas morning, I finally got my wish.

AAAA!!!

YESSS

PlayStation ™

I started playing it right away that morning and quickly became obsessed.

I had been playing video games for years, but this was the first time I had cared so deeply about the relationships between the characters. I was heavily invested.

Specifically, I had a huge crush on Cloud, the main character. But I was also very passionate about the romance between him and...

AERIS,
the flower girl?

Why did I like Aeris so much?

She had magic. She was beautiful, brave and capable. She had Cloud as her boyfriend! I wanted to be her.

I identified with Aeris. She was pretty, but very modest. We were both very sensitive. We both had brown hair. We both had February birthdays. Could I be like her someday?

I never identified with Tifa.

Part of me was jealous of her.

DEVELOPING UNIBROW

THICK GLASSES

ACNE

BRACES

ANIME T-SHIRT

NO NEED FOR A BRA

ANTI-BOY RAYS

How could a late bloomer like myself ever identify with such a sexy character? She reflected my own insecurities back at me.

As with all my obsessions at this tender age...

I decided to discuss it at length on the internet.

Welcome to Momo-Chan's Cloud + Aeris Love Shrine!!

Specifically, on forums and in chat rooms...

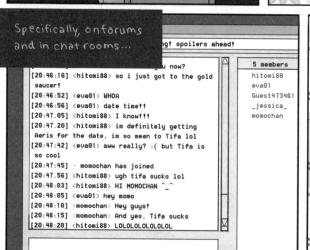

...ng! spoilers ahead!

...ou now?

[20:46:16] <hitomi88> so i just got to the gold saucer!
[20:46:52] <eva01> WHOA
[20:46:56] <eva01> date time!!
[20:47:05] <hitomi88> I know!!!
[20:47:20] <hitomi88> im definitely getting Aeris for the date, im so mean to Tifa lol
[20:47:42] <eva01> aww really? :(but Tifa is so cool
[20:47:45] - momochan has joined
[20:47:56] <hitomi88> ugh tifa sucks lol
[20:48:03] <hitomi88> HI MOMOCHAN ^_^
[20:48:05] <eva01> hey momo
[20:48:10] <momochan> Hey guys!
[20:48:15] <momochan> And yes, Tifa sucks
[20:48:20] <hitomi88> LOLOLOLOLOLOLOL

5 members
hitomi88
eva01
Guest473461
jessica
momochan

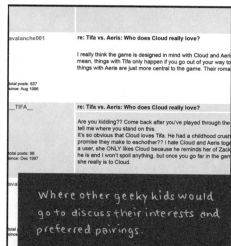

avalanche001

re: Tifa vs. Aeris: Who does Cloud really love?

I really think the game is designed in mind with Cloud and Aeris mean, things with Tifa only happen if you go out of your way to things with Aeris are just more central to the game. Their roma

total posts: 637
since: Aug 1996

__TIFA__

re: Tifa vs. Aeris: Who does Cloud really love?

Are you kidding?? Come back after you've played through the tell me where you stand on this.
It's so obvious that Cloud loves Tifa. He had a childhood crush promise they make to eachother?? i hate Cloud and Aeris toge a user, she ONLY likes Cloud because he reminds her of Zack he is and I won't spoil anything, but once you go far in the gam she really is to Cloud.

total posts: 98
since: Dec 1997

Where other geeky kids would go to discuss their interests and preferred pairings.

This was also the venue for the 'Shipping Wars'- Heated arguments over which couple was better, more true to the game and why.

NO WAY!!! it's so obvious that Cloud is still in love with AERIS!! CLOUD + AERIS 4EVER!!!11!

It's so obvious that Tifa and Cloud are together at the end! Especially since Aeris died LOL

I ship cloud with ME ^____^

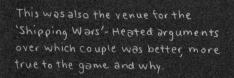

FANDOM RAGE! RAAARRR!

My extreme love for this couple was expressed in some odd ways.

MEH HEH HEH!

My website dedicated to 'Cloud + Aeris 4EVER' also included...

MUAHAHA!

...Detailed explanations on why Tifa was the worst.

I argued with my friends about it (online and off) whenever the opportunity came up.

I even refused to play with her in my party whenever possible, imagining I was insulting this digital character, somehow.

MWEH HEH HEH!

Leveling Up
Your Dating Profile

or How to Make Your Geek Shine Through

Loretta Jean

So you've finally decided get on this whole online dating thing that everyone and their mom is talking about. First off – good for you, it takes guts to put yourself out there and make yourself available to a vast sea of Internet people.

I'll probably always be the first to defend online dating as an awesome way to meet people. My primary reason is this: the Internet is the single best tool to be exposed to and meet people who share your interests and are not already in your social circle.

Meeting new people is a good thing, because when you start referring to Canada's largest fandom convention as Fan **EX**-po (I might speak from personal experience here) – you may have realized your dating type is "geeky" or "nerdy" – but dating people you already know in your local fandom or geek scene can grow tiring. Connecting with people who are entirely outside of your existing social circles is the best possible use of the technology we have available to us.

I've worked for one of the largest paid dating websites and as a dating coach for my fellow nerdy folks, giving customized advice and helping beef up their profiles. Maybe you have had some success connecting with like-minded people, or perhaps you've hit a road block or two. In either case, you probably know that the truth is that there is no magical fix or formula that will help you get more right-swipes or messages.

I want to shed some light on the best things you can do to improve your online dating profile and message response rates. Take the bits in here that resonate with you and ditch the rest. Everyone has different communication and dating styles, so feel free to adapt these suggestions to make them work for you. I offer all of this advice based on what I have observed to work for my clients who were seeking out similarly nerdily inclined partners.

What Makes You Special?

At the risk of sounding like I'm spouting too many platitudes about how awesome and special you are: you do need to own, accept and love your niche as a geek lady, whatever flavour your fandom or geeky interests might be. That might mean you are a math wiz, a comic aficionado, or a botany nerd – whatever it is for you, identify and celebrate it. Nerds and geek women (I tend to use the terms somewhat interchangeably, though I know there are many differing opinions on these terms) are as a whole, defined by our smarts (i.e. having specified knowledge or expertise) and our passion (i.e. being really invested in what we're into).

Start by writing a list of your top five to ten unique interests (the ones you think set you apart from other people or, the ones you are most passionate about) and also create a list of personal attributes or interesting facts about yourself. This isn't an exercise that needs to be taken extremely seriously, for example one of your special features might be that you won a karaoke contest at an anime convention. Being playful is encouraged, unless that doesn't come naturally to you.

As geeks we're used to taking a certain degree of teasing for our esoteric or eccentric interests. The first challenge in creating an interesting profile is to identify what makes you unique and then to highlight those attributes instead of downplaying them. The good news is that most dating sites are full of people who share your interests and get excited about the same things you do.

Specificity vs. Generality

This anthology is written for geeky women, by geeky women. We are proud of our status as people with specialized, niche interests and knowledge. Whatever it is that you choose to highlight in your profile – try to make it something that will stand out in a sea of generic declarations such as "I like eating good meals, hanging out with my friends, playing videogames, and watching movies." These types of general statements are too devoid of detail to be intriguing to anyone looking at your profile.

You might instead get specific by saying something along the lines of "My idea of a great Saturday is a sushi lunch with friends, rolling some dice with my D&D group, followed by a night at home drinking wine while playing *Dishonored* and watching *Pacific Rim*."

The idea here is strike a balance between verbosity and concision. You should give enough details to pique the interest of potential matches, but not writing a novella either – save that for NaNoWriMo.

While you do want to highlight some of your geeky interests and your personality, save the discussion of your current D&D character's stats for when it comes up in conversation. The interests or specific fandoms you highlight in your profile should be exemplary of the types of things you're into, not an exhaustive or encyclopedic list. If it helps you, maybe go the *High Fidelity* route and create some top-five lists of things that you like, but remember that at the end of the day, judging potential dates solely on their taste in media consumption is at best, a superficial measure of how compatible you will be. You'll only figure that out based on conversation and taking some time to get to know someone.

It's Not All About You

Write less about yourself and more about what you are looking for. As much as your dating profile is about making yourself seem attractive to potential dates, it's also about framing what you're looking for in a partner. If you're only looking for something casual, or perhaps something more serious – you should make sure those preferences are made known. Before actually writing your profile itself, it can be helpful to write a wish list of what you are looking for in a date. You should include some key features in your profile, so, much like an job posting, potential suitors can measure themselves up to if they have what it takes to apply for the position of being your date!

Another pointer about not making your profile entirely about yourself: try to avoid starting every sentence with "I" statements. Not only is it lazy writing, but it's boring to read and makes you sound self-centred. A well written dating profile will ideally be a mix of information about yourself and a summary of the types of people you are looking to meet.

Say Cheese

The photos you use on your profile matter more than anything else you include. Unfortunately, most people are pretty shallow and unless your photo grabs their attention they are unlikely to read what you've taken the time to write. If you're uncertain which photos to use, there's nothing wrong with asking a friend which images of you they like best.

If you do cosplay, it might be fun to throw one or two photos of yourself in costume in the mix, but those images shouldn't be the only ones on your profile. You want to show flattering but representative photos of what you actually look like. I often have told clients that you may want to also include a few where you are a tad dressed up (maybe from a family function or a special event), but at least one of the images you choose should be naturalistic and more or less what you look like every day.

This is perhaps the only absolute thing I think you need on your profile – flattering, naturally lit photographs! Even if you're semi-vampiric or deathly pale like me, indirect natural light is the most universally flattering lighting. I cannot stress this enough, unless you happen to have a professional lighting kit hanging around your home, the best selfies will always be taken in indirect natural lighting.

A photographer friend of mine once told me her clients who have acting headshots done often have a hard time picking their favourite shot. What's more, the images of us other people think are awesome of us are not always the ones we'd pick for ourselves. Her trick for fixing this is based on the fact that we're used to usually seeing ourselves in reflection. If you're having a hard time picking images of yourself for your profile, trying horizontally flipping an existing image of yourself in any image editing application. If you like the reversed image better than the original, flip it back and know the shot might be worth including after all.

If At First You Don't Succeed...

All dating can be horrible, online dating is almost never the exception to this. In some ways, you are opening yourself up to new ways that dating can suck, but it can also be a lot of fun and you can meet tons of great people too, if you're willing to put some time into the process and are willing to be patient.

If you don't meet the person of your dreams in the first week or even the first few months, don't despair. Who's to say that they won't create a profile on the site of your choice tomorrow or the day after?

More than anything, my brave friend, I want to impart upon you that online dating is only a means to an end. It is a tool to meet new people. Some people who look great online might be terrible in person and some other people who don't know how to sell themselves online, might actually be wonderful.

Try to enjoy online dating, don't feed the trolls, and above all else – have fun. As daunting as meeting new people can seem, it can also be exhilarating. Embrace the unknown and if you meet someone online who seems like they might be cool in person, try meeting up and see what happens. I'm sure I don't need to wax poetic about what should be common sense stuff (e.g. meet in a public place for your first rendezvous, telling others what your plans are ahead of time, sending a Google Maps pin to your BFF via text – whatever makes you feel safe and comfortable). In most situations, if someone isn't cool in person, you can politely excuse yourself after a bit of time both by being forthright and saying you're not feeling a connection, or making up an appropriate excuse if you absolutely must. You don't owe random strangers anything, but you owe it to yourself to give it a try.

My parting piece of advice is that if you're a woman who dates men, consider making the first move. Statistically speaking, most men usually receive a lot less messages on dating sites and apps than women do, so you're more likely to get a response than if they initiate contact. The best case scenario is you impress someone with being direct and forward rather than coy. The worst that could happen is that either they won't reply or they'll say they're not interested. Actually, regardless of the gender of who you are looking to meet, I always think it's good to make the first move if you're interested in someone. Passion (which we already know you have because you're a badass geeky lady) mixed with confidence is the sexiest combo around. Put yourself out there and maybe you'll meet someone awesome. Best of luck, my brave warrior princesses, you've got this!

Read 1:19 AM

crushing and texting with an
overactive imagination
(and maybe a little bit of anxiety)

Delivered by Jen Aprahamian

I don't even know what he texted me, but it was short enough that my brain transposed it to 😍 😍 😍

Heart eyes.

That's me right now.

I have a crush. You know what? Crushing hasn't changed one bit since the 7th grade, except that back then, you knew he'd seen the note you passed. That little paper football (which took hours to gather the nerve to compose, select the right color gel pen, and neatly craft into a compact triangle) would unfold in seconds, before your eyes, and with it, the story of that crush would unfold, too. Immediate response. IRL heart eyes. Cool rejection. It didn't matter, there was no suspense at all, and the crush could be promoted to full-blown infatuation or dismissed in a blink.

Somehow, our more mature selves have traded this simple situation for something much more angst-inducing. Instead of laboring over each letter, we dash them off in a matter of seconds. Send, send, send, who cares how it's spelled, blame autocorrect for your carelessness to mask the anxiety of interacting with someone you're crushing on, accidentally tap the phone call button and hang up in a flurry of embarrassment because you're not at the talking stage yet.

So, it's kind of a mess.

I'm kind of a mess.

I glance at my phone again, and it just says *delivered*. There's no read receipt. This is me throwing the football-note with my eyes shut and not even knowing if he opened it or not.

I panic. I fire off three texts in succession. Rapid-fire.

He texted me 😍😍😍

!! What did he say?

Doesn't matter. He's cute 😊

What do I say? I want to sound interesting!

Don't say anything.
Wait for him to start
the conversation.

What. Too late.
Already texted a
million things.

Okay three.

You're cut off at three.
Wait for him so you
don't look too
available.

How long am I
supposed to wait?

It's been ages.

It's been 20 minutes.

Be cool.

I AM NOT COOL. I
HAVE A CRUSH

How do I even know if
he likes me back?

He texted you. He
likes you.

He texted once!

TODAY. Didn't he blow
up your phone for 8
hours the other day?

Chill. Let it play out.

He is DREAMY 😍

He'd be dreamier if I
knew he liked me.

Why did I just do that? What did I even say? Did I sound clever or make a good joke or even say something worth responding to? Gosh, he's got great arms, I hope he texts back so I can find a way to compliment them.

Am I texting too much? He's so cute; I'm probably coming on too strong. I text my best friend to confirm. I've sent her 65 messages in the last 4 minutes, so the three I just sent to him are nothing.

Or *are* they nothing? He hasn't read them yet.

My best friend explains The Rules to me, and I fight the urge to send yet another text -- because maybe if I send something especially interesting, he'll suddenly feel inspired to read it, even though he hasn't gotten around to opening the other ones -- and instead bemoan the lack of specificity of delivery receipts. *Delivered.* Delivered is useless. Delivered only tells me that the technology didn't fail here, but delivered doesn't do a single thing to temper my angst. Delivered just has a time stamp, nothing else I need.

Delivered 3:31 p.m.

Delivered 3:31 p.m.

Delivered, possibly seen 3:39 p.m.

Delivered, definitely seen 3:56 p.m.

Totally seen, right? 5:12 p.m.

Seen, ignored, willfully allowing a badge to stay open on phone just to not read 5:29 p.m.

Seen, ignored, badges piling up, tweeting, not reading 6:01 p.m.

Tweeting "I'm bored" missives and still not reading this text 9:44 p.m.

This is ludicrous. I should put down my phone.

I mean, I can't really put down my phone...someone important might need to reach me.

He might need to reach me.

I need to be cool. I need to be cool and detach. I need to be cool and detach and know that the phone will be waiting for me and maybe a text will arrive later.

I distract myself -- or try to -- but crushes are crushes, and even as I do work, make coffee, read an article, catch up with a friend, it's more like do work (check phone) make coffee (check phone) read an article (check phone four times, don't finish article, it's boring and there might be a text) catch up with a friend (check phone, gush about how cute he is, ask friend's opinion about him, check phone again).

I'm losing it. I need reinforcements.

My friend has a crush too, and we exchange giggles and talk about how silly it is that we haven't grown out of these utterly consuming infatuations yet. This is 7th grade stuff, isn't it, but here we are, dissecting the read receipts, trying to determine whether it's them (maybe) or us (definitely) or we're reading too much into it (yes, one hundred percent, absolutely).

We try to figure out if we're handling this well, and become our very own tailor-made echo chamber of *You're totally fine. He's definitely into you.* and *Women just like to communicate more, so it's not weird that you're sending 4 messages for every one of his.* and *Oh honey, I Facebook-stalked him for you, and you're prettier than his ex, so you have nothing to worry about.* and by the end of the conversation it's not even clear which "he" and which "you" are the subjects anymore.

I try not to check my phone again -- because I'm totally chill and totally sympathetic to whatever situation is keeping him from reading those texts -- and make it a full sixteen minutes before trying to draft something witty to send.

Then I see it.

● ● ●

Three animated dots. He's typing. *Oh my stars, he's typing.* Everything is okay in the world, he's typing.

He stops. Why did he stop?

Has he texted you yet?

No.

☹

He will. I promise.

I don't know. He hasn't even read my messages from before. Maybe this crush is one-sided?

There's no way.

Maybe he's working.

WE'RE working

No, we're talking about boys. He might be actually working.

He hasn't even tweeted all day.

You're right.

Maybe something is wrong.

WAIT. I see the 3 dots, he's typing...

What did he say?

Nothing. That was 20 minutes ago, but he never sent anything.

Maybe he's busy.

Too busy to hit send on a message he already typed?

Nobody is that busy unless their house is on fire.

OH MY GOD, THAT HAS TO BE IT. HIS HOUSE IS ON FIRE.

I can't help but let my imagination take over. It's not enough to accept completely rational explanations for why that reply never arrived. His phone isn't dead. He's not fighting a deadline. He isn't napping.

You see, these explanations are too simple. He is not simple. I do not have heart-eyes over simple.

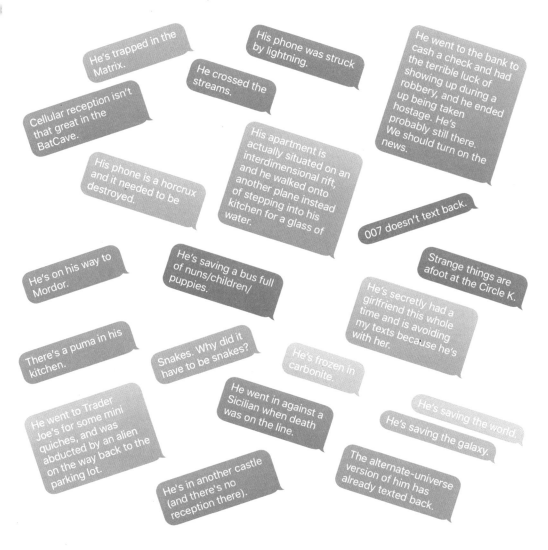

The only obvious conclusion is that his house is on fire and he stopped typing mid-text because he passed out from smoke inhalation (and not at all because he has something else to do besides text me) and his life is in danger and I really oughta call the fire department...

• • •

Wait...it's the dots again!

He's alive!

(I knew it.)

And he's texting ME!

(Of course he is, I'm a swell lady.)

I wonder what he has to say! Did he see my joke or question or
whatever it was earlier?

I need a new crush...

Mashing Our Buttons: On Romance and Sex in Videogames

Soha Kareem

I take romance in videogames seriously.

I dated this guy; let's call him Connor. We had the type of relationship where I mistook our cyclical toxic drama for a tragic we-love-each-other-*just-too-much* story out of a Lana del Rey album. I introduced him to BioWare's *Mass Effect*, a sci-fi franchise about saving the galaxy, befriending aliens, and sometimes getting the chance to smooch the aliens.

When it comes to romance options, *Mass Effect*'s writers earn the praise they receive by creating thoughtful tensions between the protagonist and a number of non-playable characters. Not all tensions are created equally, however, a feeling confirmed as I watched Connor closely while he interacted with potential loves.

I watched him start to make the moves on Miranda Lawson, a boring femme-fatale type whose screentime includes opportunistic angles on her ass. She was artificially created by her father who aimed to make an "ideal woman." I remember my eyelids closing in toward each other in an embittered squint.

Of course he would pick Miranda.

Miranda is pretentious. Miranda is a product of wealth and

masculine power structures. Miranda would write the space version of Sheryl Sandberg's *Lean In.*

Miranda Lawson kind of sucks.

This point is exacerbated with how terribly she treats Jack, a member of your crew who was kidnapped, experimented on, and tortured her entire life since childhood.

As I saw Connor woo Miranda and gaslight Jack, I knew that our days were numbered. To be fair, that relationship should've ended before it started, but watching him recreate himself and his desires in this game legitimized my growing resentment of him.

Listen, I take romance in videogames *seriously.*

Unlike BioWare, Bethesda's games don't build up as sophisticated relationships with meaningful interactions, often treating love and sex as a garnish.

It's quite disappointing to compare the romance plots between BioWare and Bethesda games since both studios are known for creating large role-playing games with hundreds of possibilities; the former progresses important arcs and the latter fumbles with one-dimensional personalities.

In Bethesda's *Skyrim*, you wear a bronze amulet with turquoise accents and approach non-playable characters in order to add a dialogue option about marriage. If you've already completed a sidequest for them, they'll say yes. Boom! Now you're married, and they can live in your house and make you meals, and their dialogue doesn't change regardless of how many missions you complete or difficult choices you make.

In *Fallout: New Vegas* however, romance is underhanded even where sex workers and heartfelt companions exist throughout the Mojave Wasteland. Unless you consider being fisted by a robot (named Fisto) or laying next to a woman in bed as romance options, you won't be able to develop an intimate relationship with anyone, which is increasingly frustrating during an add-on to the game titled *Dead Money*.

Dead Money revolves around *Fallout: New Vegas'* protagonist, nicknamed the Courier, being lured into visiting the Sierra Madre, a city within the Mojave Wasteland that's become a legend. It contains the Sierra Madre Casino, which was set to open until a nuclear apocalypse named the Great War changed the world forever. The city's advanced security went into lockdown-mode, sealing guests and civilians inside the Madre, who all began slowly dying and descending into a dystopia plagued by extreme radiation and red clouds of poisonous gas.

The Madre became an obsession to many, and the only person who reached the city after its lockdown is a man named Father Elijah, who then traps the Courier and three others to open the casino and retrieve all the gold within it. One of the characters the Courier meets is a woman named Christine Royce, and I completely fell in love with her.

Christine was brought to the Madre while tracking down Elijah to bring him to justice after he committed a series of crimes within the Wasteland in order to find the Madre. When the Courier meets her, she's just had her vocal cords removed and has to use sign language. If you've worked on your Speech and Intelligence skills throughout the game, the Courier is able to read her signs clearly and finds that she is after Elijah for an additional reason—he separated her from her lover, a woman named Veronica Santangelo. At this point, you can hear my female Courier internally screaming about Christine being into women.

In one mission during *Dead Money*, you station the others lured into the Madre with you at different points on the map in order to complete the perfect heist. If your character has been able to read Christine's signs during interactions, she hesitantly reaches out her hand to you before you leave her at her station. You can then choose to reach your hand back out to her, and the game prompts, "She holds it, meeting your eyes intently for a few moments. She gives your hand a gentle squeeze, then releases it and smiles slightly." You tell her you'll come back for her, and then walk away to complete preparations for the heist.

In the moments where I've wanted to kiss a videogame character on the spot, this is easily in my top 5.

By the end of *New Vegas'* plot, Christine regains her voice, and no option opens to romance her or hold her hand again. The Courier leaves the Madre and exits through a bunker with a radio broadcast playing on loop. Christine's sad yet hopeful voice fills the silent room, saying, "Wait a moment, before you go, I…we hope you've enjoyed your stay. Farewells can be a time of sadness, letting go…difficult. I hope you'll return, in happier times. Until then the Sierra Madre, and I, will hold you in our hearts."

The state of my heartbreak worsens when later in the game I meet the lover she was separated from, Veronica, in the Mojave Wasteland. Veronica is one of the few characters in *New Vegas* who can be a companion, meaning you can take her along on missions, share an inventory, and be badass gal pals in the desert shooting at various enemies and monsters. Although it's not explicitly stated that Veronica is Christine's long lost love, there is enough evidence in your conversations with her and data found in journals to suggest that's the case.

As you spend more time with her, you learn that one of Veronica's desires is to wear a pretty dress. She usually wears a bland, brown hooded robe, or armor if you've chosen to equip her with it. On a mission, I found a pink dress that I thought she might like, and popped it into her inventory. She squealed with joy, excited about being able to wear a dress, and teaches you a skill in return to improve your combat. I paused the game, needing a moment to emotionally digest how happy Christine would've been if she was with you, if you were able to convince her to leave the Sierra Madre and come to the Wasteland to reunite with Christine. The thought of Christine watching Veronica happily twirl in her new dress while wielding a shotgun basically tore me to pieces.

The disappointment I feel is layered: I can't romance Christine, I can't romance Veronica, I can't reunite them, or even acknowledge their relationship to them. I could tell Veronica that I met Father Elijah, the man responsible for the women's time apart, and yet can't mention that Christine was with me too. To be frank, coding extra dialogue wouldn't have been a problem. Game design has a lot of cause and effect codes, usually in the form of "if X happens, then Y happens." I just wanted to put my hand on Veronica's shoulder and say, "I found Christine, and she still loves you, and you can see her at the Madre. It's safe to visit now." For games as large as Bethesda's, it's increasingly frustrating to be given a carrot on a stick and yearn for what potentially could be a beautiful relationship or dynamic intimacy.

Not many games take romance seriously, and even BioWare who I've heralded as treating love narratively well, have failed me a few times during my romance with an alien named Thane Krios in *Mass Effect 2* and *3* (but that's an entirely different chapter for another time). Unless a developer is strictly making a dating simulator, romance can feel like an afterthought as writers awkwardly bash two character models into each other to attempt a realistic sex scene.

This is disheartening; a well-written plot about characters falling in love with each other is one of the strongest ways to build connections and create a feeling that exists outside the game's designs. I've spent many nights, perhaps too many, scrounging Tumblr posts to find others who feel the same way about the one true pairs I've allowed to take up room in my headspace. There are always communities built around the need of having and cherishing an OTP, expressing how stories can be improved or created – a validating feeling which simultaneously pushes my frustrations further. So many of us *desperately want these romances, so where the fuck are they!*

Until gamemakers commit to the plots that make my heart swell, I guess there will always be fanfiction.

Like alot of people my age, I've had to come to terms with having low self-esteem.

Most of all with romance.

A problem compounded by my talent for misreading friend signals as romantic.

HIGH SCHOOL

ONE

WORK

AFTER

COLLEGE

ANOTHER

WORK

Online dating helped alot by taking out the guess work. I knew why guys were talking to me and vice versa.

And, to be fair, you get alot more attention as a girl.

ACT II - THE FATHER OF DEATH

PROTOMEN

Then, I ran into regular dating problems. Either I didn't like them...

I don't GET having a dog.

They just DIE.

"A human that breathes the same air as us.

Or they didn't like me.

YOU'VE NEVER HEARD OF BEAST WARS???? OMG DEAD TO ME

4 days ag

Hey, free tuesday?

5 days

I got gun shy and would only date a couple times a year

gammagrrl last logged on two months

This went on for a few years.

I still <u>went</u> on dates, mind you.

But I'd built a troubling defense mechanism.

TAP TAP

The best way I can describe it is that it prevented me from getting my hopes up.

It operated on these rules:

- make sure to be busy with work beforehand (prevent pre-jitters)

- Don't try hard with appearance

- give self an out to go back to work ('I'm on deadline, I can only do 2 hrs')

And this worked.

Not with getting a boyfriend, but the process became a lot less emotionally exhausting.

I started dating more.

gammagrrl
last logged on
two days ago

Then, one night I had a date scheduled at a Starbucks near my studio space.

PROTOMEN

And I was doing my best to care as little as possible.

bare minimum makeup

comfy hoody

tumblr

work

birthday cake

125

I'm Your Biggest Fan

Adrienne Kress

I'm not a very good artist. But this didn't stop me from drawing one of the only comics I ever attempted. It was in my diary. It was of my grade six crush asking me out. My ideal being-asked-out scenario.

My crush never did ask me out.

I'm glad.

He could never have lived up to those six panels.

"How many geeks does it take to screw in a lightbulb…?"

One evening, not too long ago, I was chatting with a friend of mine. She was bemoaning the fact that she really didn't know how to relationship. Or (to make it even less commitment-y) how to date. My friend would totally like someone, but then, once she'd actually date that someone, she would feel wrong, uncomfortable. And almost as soon as it had begun, she'd end it.

"Yes!" I agreed a bit too vehemently. "I know exactly that feeling! I too have had these huge epic crushes on boys, and then they'd ask me out, and then I'd want them to go away!"

As I was speaking, I had a lightbulb moment. "We're fans!" I said. Then I had to explain, because it was a bit of an outburst. "I mean, we're fans of shows and books and characters and actors. But we are so used to being fans that we've become fans of our crushes too!"

And how could any crush live up to the expectations placed on them by fandom?

"And now for something completely different."

Fun fact: my dad read me all of *Lord of the Rings*. ALL of it. ALL... well actually, I now think he cut a great deal of the Council of Elrond, but I mean I think he made the right choice considering his audience consisted of one solitary ten-year-old more interested in adventure than politics (and who was already righteously indignant there weren't enough girl characters).

My dad read me all of *Lord of the Rings* and did the voices, and we spent the entirety of one storytime trying to remember how my dad used to read Bilbo's voice when we met up with him again in Rivendell.

When the movies were about to come out, he and I went to see the exhibit of the costumes and props at Casa Loma. And we saw the first screening of the first movie together.

The question of whether it was nature or nurture that fueled my nerdity is still up in the air.

"I'm your biggest fan!"

"You're right!" my friend said.

"I know!" (I'm nothing if not modest.) "It all makes sense! We place these crushes on pedestals; we create in our heads a kind of fanfiction of us with them, perfect romantic situations where everything goes flawlessly. We totally Mary Sue ourselves! But the difference between a real-life-person crush, and a crush on, say, Benedict Cumberbatch, is that we never actually meet Benedict Cumberbatch (though I hold onto my hope and, FYI, am still hoping). I mean, if we did meet Benedict Cumberbatch we'd probably end up having the same discomfort as we have with the crushes in our lives who actually reciprocate: 'Agh! He's human! He has flaws! This feels very, very, very uncomfortable!'"

(Uh, of course, Mr. Cumberbatch, I mean all this in the most flattering way, I write, assuming you'll actually read this.)

The thing is, there's a safety and security in crushing on celebrities or the characters they play because deep down we know we'll never meet them. And therefore they can never disappoint us. But holding people in our real lives up to the same standard gets problematic.

"Great! Where're we goin'?"

It was only after the first *Lord of the Rings* movie came out that I discovered other people aside from me and my dad who were fans of it. And there was a particular group of us who bonded over our obsession with it. We all attended drama school together, and we all loved Legolas. In fact, Legolas is responsible for our little group's very first Internet purchase ever: T-shirts that read "Legolas Lives in my Heart." I still have mine. It's a white baby-T. I love it.

But something happened. As the subsequent films came out, and while I still adored Legolas and thought Aragorn was just plain dreamy, I started to fall for someone completely unexpected.

Pippin. As played by the delightful Scottish actor Billy Boyd.

Falling for a Hobbit was unusual in a movie that featured such spectacularly stereotypically manly men. But hey, the heart wants what the heart wants, and my heart wanted a "fool of a Took."

Something else also happened. I found that there was no one in my day-to-day life for me to crush on. And so, for the first time ever, I transferred real-world crush feelings onto a film actor. Now, I'd had film actor crushes before, but they were very pragmatic. They weren't real crushes like I had on people around me. They were, "Ooh isn't he cute!" and the answer to the teen version of "What's your favourite colour?" – "Who's your actor crush?" But the crush I developed on Mr. Boyd was big. And suddenly I understood my peers so much better. The ones who were single-minded in their love of one particular celebrity, covering their walls with pictures, who couldn't talk about anyone else.

But the biggest revelation of all was I realized that I'd been crushing on real-life people the way people crush on celebrities. I never assumed anything would come of a crush on a real person, just as we assume nothing will come of a celebrity crush. We hope, I mean, we hope... but we rely on the premise that, ultimately, no real contact will ever happen.

I was relying on none of these real-life crushes ever actually turning into relationships.

Despite wanting a boyfriend, I was scared of the reality of having a boyfriend.

"Houston, we have a problem."

Now there are two possible outcomes for holding people up to an impossible standard.

1. No one can live up to that standard so you are constantly disappointed in them.

2. You are so invested in the standard that you don't notice that the person is not at all as perfect as you'd like them to be and so excuse certain rather unpleasant behaviours or pretend not to notice them. This is the one that can have actual dangerous ramifications.

I was, fortunately, in the first group. "Fortunately" because it meant I had managed to avoid being taken advantage of or staying in an unhealthy relationship in the hope it would all work out. But unfortunately this fan-ing of my crushes translated into a pretty lousy love life for a good long while. You see, none of the guys I dated could live up to the expectations I had. They were real people, not fantasies. They were fallible and couldn't read my mind. And for this reason the relationships, if you could even call them that, were over almost as soon as they'd begun.

These boys weren't to blame for any of this. But it nonetheless took a very long time for me to come to terms with the fact that my crushes were, in fact, human beings.

"Run away!!"

Several years back I directed a play I had written. We presented it at the Edinburgh Festival Fringe, our venue a converted boardroom in a rather swanky hotel.

I showed up early for the show one evening. I walked into the hotel. And there, checking in, was Billy Boyd.

I stared.

Now here's what I could have done: I could have approached him politely and said, "Hi, Mr. Boyd? I just wanted to say I'm a big fan and I don't want to bother you, but I'm the playwright and director of a play that's happening in half an hour upstairs, and here's a postcard with information about it, and if you have the time, maybe you might want to check it out. Of course I totally understand that you're likely very busy."

He might have replied with, "Marry me."

But instead, I ran away.

"Worst. Crushing. Ever."

I have done nothing so many times with real-life crushes. I avoided asking out a lot of guys, many of whom (I discovered far too late) actually liked me too. And I have done it on purpose. I consciously avoided the real opportunities for fear they would not live up to my expectations. And also, quite frankly, because I worried I wouldn't know what to do in the real-life situations. In my fantasies, I say all the right things. I never blush, I'm never tongue tied. My Mary Sue self is all the best parts of me. There is no self doubt and there is certainly no question of what his feelings are for me.

I avoided the reality of having a real-world boyfriend, because deep, deep down I liked the fantasy better. And when I finally did date someone I found that the fantasy was indeed much easier. It was safer, it was predictable, it was what I wanted the way I wanted it.

Most of all, I was what I wanted to be.

"Make it so."

How do we who fan our crushes stop doing so?

Well, the first step is acknowledging the problem. That tends to be the first step in most things. Except when it's a step on a staircase. But even then: I acknowledge the problem here is that the ground is no longer flat.

And then we have to be a bit more accepting of others – but not so much so that we are too accepting of everything. How do we know the difference between a regular flaw and a Shakespearean tragic flaw? That's trickier. Maybe the number of "thou"s…

But I think the most important step is to be vulnerable. To put ourselves out there. To have a little more trust in others that they will like us, warts (metaphorical or not) and all. To be, ultimately, accepting of ourselves.

We need to be a little braver.

Step outside of our comfort zone.

Feel uncomfortable, but know it isn't a forever feeling.

We need to start making our way up to the second floor, where the ground will be flat again, if only for a little while.

A solid relationship is about two people trusting each other. About two people complementing each other. Not just one person putting all their hopes into someone else. Because no one can live up to that.

No one's perfect.

I'm not perfect.

It's about two imperfect people coming together and going, "Hey you're cool, I like spending time with you. Let's spend more time together."

And then maybe turning on *Lord of the Rings* and fan-ing out over it together.

WHEN I WAS A KID, THERE WAS ONE QUESTION I DREADED ABOVE ALL OTHERS

ONE FOR WHICH THERE WAS NO OTHER ANSWER THAN...

DO YOU like Me?

YES

NO

MAYBE

story & art by
Megan Kearney

IT'S REALLY INTERESTING JUST HOW MANY OF OUR PLAYGROUND GAMES CENTRE AROUND MATCH-MAKING

PICK A COLOUR!

OK, SO YOU'LL LIVE IN A MANSION...YOU'LL MARRY MARCUS... AND YOU'LL HAVE TEN KIDS...

A...B....C...D....E...F! F...I'M GONNA MARRY FRANÇOISE?

SNAP

RICH MAN, POOR MAN, BEGGAR MAN, THIEF....

SKIP
SKIP

AT MY SCHOOL, THERE WAS EVEN AN ELITE TEAM OF FAST, CONFIDENT GIRLS WHO WOULD CHASE DOWN THE BOYS AND THEN SMOOCH THEIR UNLUCKY PREY.

THEY WERE CALLED "THE KISSING GIRLS"

WAUUUGH!

I WAS NOT ONE OF THEM.

NO, I WAS AGGRESSIVELY DISINTERESTED IN ALL THINGS MUSHY. I TOOK MY COOTIE SHOT VERY SERIOUSLY.

CIRCLE, CIRCLE, DOT, DOT, NOW YOU'VE GOT A COOTIE SHOT...

CIRCLE, CIRCLE, SQUARE, SQUARE, NOW YOU'VE GOT IT EVERYWHERE.

e Me?

ES

(as a friend)

NO

MAYBE

EVEN AS A KID, I KNEW THERE WAS NO EASY WAY TO ESCAPE THIS QUESTION. MY STRATEGY WAS TO PLAY DUMB AND THEN AVOID MY POOR ADMIRER FOR THE REST OF THE YEAR.

OK, KEARNEY. YOU EITHER FIND SOMEONE THIS YEAR, OR YOU START BUYING CATS.

HE SEEMS... POLITE.

IN GRAD SCHOOL, I DECIDED I HAD TO GET SERIOUS. BUT IT WAS HARD! I DIDN'T KNOW WHAT KIND OF CRITERIA PEOPLE USED TO DECIDE IF SOMEONE WAS ATTRACTIVE OR NOT.

WHEN I DID FIND A BOYFRIEND, I WAS STILL A LITTLE BIT JUMPY.

I--I--I-- THIS KISSING THING, LOOK, I D-DONT KNOW--

HEY, SLOW IS OK. SLOW IS FINE.

I THINK I COULD REALLY USE SLOW RIGHT NOW.

BUT HE WAS PRETTY COOL ABOUT IT.

.....THOUGH NOT EVERYONE I KNEW WAS SO UNDERSTANDING. I WAS TRYING HARD TO PUSH MY BOUNDARIES, BUT THAT WASN'T ENOUGH FOR NOSY PEERS.

HE'S GOING TO LEAVE YOU IF YOU DON'T FUCK HIM, YOU KNOW.

LOOK, YOU'RE GONNA HAVE TO SOONER OR LATER. JUST GET IT OVER WITH.

YOU USED TO SEEM COOL BUT YOURE REALLY SCREWED UP

I MEAN, WHAT'S WRONG WITH YOU?

SERIOUSLY, YOU HAVE TO PAY HIM BACK FOR ALL THE STUFF HE DOES FOR YOU.

B-BUT I C-CAN'T! WE'VE ONLY BEEN GOING OUT A YEAR!

I DON'T W-WANT TO BE ALONE AGAIN!

B-BUT I DON'T KNOW IF I LOVE HIM!

IT MESSED ME UP.

WHEN WE FINALLY TALKED ABOUT WHY I WAS SO UPSET, HIS RESPONSE SURPRISED ME

THIS IS **OUR** RELATIONSHIP, AND **OUR** CHOICES

IT WAS TRUE, I HAD A LOT OF BAGGAGE.

IT TOOK A LONG TIME FOR ME TO TRUST THAT MY OWN BOYFRIEND WASN'T GOING TO LEAVE ME, GET FED UP WITH ME, OR MAKE A JOKE OF ME.

HEY!

BAM

AND WHEN THAT CAREFULLY CONSTRUCTED WALL AROUND MY HEART FINALLY CAME DOWN, I FELL SO HARD FOR HIM IT WAS DIZZYING

I SPENT A LOT OF MY ADOLESCENCE TRYING TO COME UP WITH SOME SORT OF EXPLANATION THAT WOULD GET PEOPLE OFF MY BACK

OH, I'M... UH... SORTA RELIGIOUS?

I'M A ROMANTIC, I GUESS?

I'M VERY FOCUSED ON SCHOOL.

I'M JUST KINDA OLD-FASHIONED.

THERE WAS SO MUCH SOCIAL, PARENTAL AND MEDIA PRESSURE TO LIKE SOMEONE,

SO WHEN I WAS FARTING AROUND ONLINE AND CAME ACROSS THE DEFINITION OF "DEMISEXUAL" ...

Demisexual
dɛmiˈsɛkʃʊəl/

Demisexuality is characterized b
lack of sexual or romantic attracti
except in the case of a strong emo
connection with a specific partner

124 notes

THIS IS A THING?!

IT WAS LIKE FINALLY ARRIVING AT THE SOLUTION TO A PUZZLE

NOWADAYS WE HAVE LOTS OF RESOURCES REGARDING THE ASEXUAL AND AROMANTIC SPECTRUM, I'M NOT A BIG FAN OF LABELS, SO I THINK OF THIS SORT OF THING NOT AS AN IDENTITY TO ASSUME, BUT AS A WAY TO DESCRIBE A PATTERN OF BEHAVIOUR

BUT, GEEZE!! JUST KNOWING THERE WAS A WORD FOR PEOPLE WHO FEEL OR ACT LIKE THIS WOULD HAVE SPARED BABY-ME A LOT OF SELF-DOUBT AND PAIN!

WHEN YOU CAN CLASSIFY SOMETHING, IT HELPS PIN IT DOWN INTO A THING YOU CAN HANDLE INSTEAD OF A NAMELESS DREAD.

IT TOOK ME A LONG TIME TO OVERCOME AMBIVALENCE AND FEAR TO LET MYSELF BE VULNERABLE

I'M HAPPY TO FINALLY BE ABLE TO CHECK A BOX.

How Fanfic from an American Girl Captured an English Boy

Megan Lavey-Heaton, illustration by Isabelle Melançon

This story has a happy ending.

I'm writing it in the living room, with one cat curled beneath my feet and two more asleep on the couch. Behind me, my husband laughs at YouTube videos before he gets up to change out the laundry and try to sneak in an hour of *Destiny* before work. On the shelf next to him, his Batman and my *Doctor Who* knickknacks need dusting. A stack of graphic novels sit in my office waiting to be read, and comic pages are on my iMac needing to be lettered as my long-suffering creative partner reminds me of my *Secret Loves of Geek Girls* deadline.

I might be checking out my husband's ass as he takes care of the laundry. I know he'll be checking out mine as I get ready for work. We'll flirt with each other as if we've been married five minutes rather than five years.

When I walk back into the living room after getting dressed, he looks at me as if he can't believe I'm in his life. When I look back, it's with the same expression.

Fandom in 2005 was coming into its own. We were in mid-*Harry Potter* mania. Attendance at conventions was growing, and so were places like LiveJournal and Fanfiction.net. When I began reading *Ranma 1/2* in 1995, manga barely took up a shelf in the comics section of the bookstore. Now it was its own section. We were on the cusp of the social media revolution, only years away from Facebook and Twitter.

That year, I was working as a visual journalist in Lewiston, Maine. It was a great spot to raise a family, but a terrible place to be single, geeky, and in your mid-20s. I was home sick from work when I got an email from a reader. For years, I would lie and say this was an email from someone who found my journalism work online. But this reader was actually one of many who enjoyed my *Slayers* fanfiction.

I'd been writing fanfic at that point on a steady basis for 10 years, scribbling stories about Dr. Michaela Quinn, Tsukino Usagi, Himura Kenshin, Inuyasha, and now Lina Inverse. I wrote whenever I could, filling pages of a notebook with Sailor Moon fanfic when I was supposed to be paying attention to my classes in college. I alternated between interviewing people at my newspaper jobs and arguing character motivations on LiveJournal. I would design a newspaper page as quickly as possible so I could appease my muse in the 15 minutes I had to wait on the next one.

I wasn't always comfortable with this. Fanfiction writing wasn't as mainstream at it is now, and especially once you reached the professional world, you kept it under wraps. I attended journalism workshops, networked for promotions, and didn't dare breathe that in my spare time I crafted new adventures for an animated sorceress and her bodyguard that just might involve sex.

A virgin until I was 24, my first sexual relationship was with a fellow journalist. He took pity on my lesser salary and bought me a laptop, my first iPod, and gave me $40 every week to spend on what I wanted. I always took advantage of the buy-3, get-1 free sales at Waldenbooks to increase my manga collection. He thought that my manga reading phase was cute, and that once we were married, I would grow out of it.

That relationship lasted six months.

Back to that email. I wish I could tell you what it exactly said, other than the reader enjoyed my work. I do remember it was a longer note than normal and very sweet. So, I did what my mother taught me to do – I wrote back. And the reader replied. I realized this was a guy, a relatively rare thing in the Lina/Gourry fandom. Curious, I found his LiveJournal and a very bad webcam picture of him. I wrinkled my nose, said, "Ew," and closed the browser.

Sorry, sweetie.

After having undergone a bad breakup with the fellow journalist, I didn't want to deal with men. But that reader, KawaiiGourry666, kept writing and eventually began to instant message me. About 70% of me did not want to respond. However, the discussions were nice and just about *Slayers*, so I kept writing back. I learned that KawaiiGourry666 had a thing for another person in the fandom that he dated virtually for a time, so I relaxed further. He wanted nothing from me other than to chat about our OTP.

I decided to try dating again in 2006. I subscribed to eHarmony and

Match.com and on the surface was everything their typical match process wanted: a college-educated woman with a good job. But when I discussed my love for *World of Warcraft* or my new Wii with the potential dates, a wall of silence answered back.

I'm the woman who at one point could recite the title of every episode and original airdate of *Dr. Quinn, Medicine Woman* by memory. I wrote fanfic every chance I could get and had at least a hundred works to my name spread out among several archives. I watched as people got paired off around me and cried from aching loneliness at 2 am, convinced that there was no one out there that would accept me for who I was.

It was during those lonely nights that KawaiiGourry666 and I started spending hours chatting. He was eight hours ahead of me in England, and he was just as lonely as I was. He was equally convinced that no woman would accept him for who he was. Mike, his real name, became one of my best friends. He loved *Slayers*, Batman, videogames and shipped Lina/Gourry and Batman/Catwoman. He was getting a PhD in astrophysics and was endearingly shy. He thought the worst of himself and the best of me. I thought the worst of myself and the best of him.

In January 2007, I went on a second date with a man I'd met on Match.com. As I ate my salad, the man proceeded to tell me that he knew from the moment we met that we were soulmates.

"Why can't you be like my friend Mike?" I thought.

Uh oh.

By that fall, Mike had realized his once-online girlfriend wouldn't return his feelings. I had attempted a long-distance relationship with a guy in Wisconsin that I met through anime forums, trying to convince myself that I was not crushing on a guy in England, that a relationship with him was impossible.

When that spectacularly failed, I finally bared my heart to Mike, in tears the entire time. *I have a crush on you*, I wrote. *I'm sorry.* I was convinced our friendship was about to end.

Mike took a day to respond and finally acknowledged that he had a crush on me too. A month and an ocean liner of sexual tension later, we decided to give a relationship a shot.

The odds were stacked against us. There's no scientific study that I could find that gave a number for sure, but conventional wisdom and our own experience led us to believe that we'd have six weeks at the most. Our friends were skeptical, our families were clueless. We would use Skype and our imaginations to deal with this attraction and move on with our lives.

Dating Mike was the easiest thing I'd ever done. We met in person for the first time six months after we became a couple, when we attended Anime North in Toronto. When I picked him up from the airport, I wasn't quite sure what to do with him. That night, I gave him a hug and he started to walk away. I then called him back, tugged him to me, and kissed him senseless.

I knew I loved him when I walked out of the bathroom to find him checking in on an Amazon order. My Scouser, who loathed Microsoft products, had purchased an Xbox 360 for a children's hospital and donated it without saying a word to me or anyone else. With a heart as big as his, how could I not fall in love?

We got engaged after a year of dating. This happened after a harrowing flight where the plane had to make an emergency landing in Atlanta. The thought of me getting home to tell Mike I wanted to marry him kept me sane.

When we'd been together two years, he had a mini-stroke, which led him to having heart surgery at age 26. Three weeks after surgery, he flew through a blizzard to surprise me for my 30th birthday. We married four days later. 20 months after our marriage, PhD in hand, he immigrated to the United States.

In the early stages of our relationship, I convinced Mike to cosplay Batman, something he'd always wanted to do and was too afraid of rejection to do so. I love it every time he puts on his costume. Someday, at some convention, you might see a comic writer walk out from behind her table, tug a Batman to her, snog the hell out of him, and pinch his ass beneath his cape.

THEY BURY YOU IN WHITE

BY LAURA NEUBERT

I DON'T KNOW **EXACTLY** HOW THIS FEAR DEVELOPED.

BUT IT WAS **ALWAYS** THERE.

EEEEE!

MARRIAGE IN STORIES **FRIGHTENED** ME TERRIBLY.

OH, **LET'S DATE** FOREVERRR!

EVEN IN PLAY, I AVOIDED IT.

AS I GREW **OLDER**, I LEARNED SOMETHING ABOUT FUNERALS.

IT RESONATED **HEAVILY** WITH MY FEARS.

IN SOME PLACES, **THEY BURY YOU IN WHITE.**

IN **FICTION**, GIRLS' ROLES ARE LIMITED.

THIS STARTS **VERY** EARLY.

THESE OPTIONS **APPEAR** DIVERSE.

REALLY, THEY'RE **SIMPLE.**

LET'S BREAK THEM DOWN.

THE MAIDEN/INGENUE
(ALSO KNOWN AS 'THE GIRL')

TO HAVE AN **ADVENTURE** AND **RELEVANCY,**

YOU NEED TO BE PRETTY, YOUNG, **ROMANTICALLY AVAILABLE** AND CHILDLESS.

THE WITCH/HAG/FEMME FATALE

EVIL WOMEN ARE USUALLY UNATTACHED, **BITTER,** AND OVER TWENTY.

THEY CAN'T BE REDEEMED. JUST DESTROYED.

THERE'S ALMOST AN IMPLICATION THAT OLDER WOMEN RESENT WHAT THEY HAVE LOST.

THERE'S EXCEPTIONS, BUT...

NOT ENOUGH TO **EASE** MY FEARS.

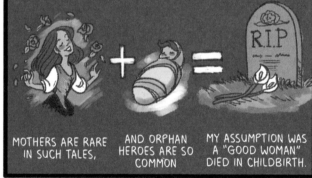

MOTHERS ARE RARE IN SUCH TALES,

AND ORPHAN HEROES ARE SO COMMON

MY ASSUMPTION WAS A "GOOD WOMAN" DIED IN CHILDBIRTH.

REALITY WASN'T LIKE THAT.

I KNEW MANY DYNAMIC, **COOL** WOMEN.

NONE FIT A MAIDEN/HAG DYNAMIC.

BUT, TO PARAPHRASE A POPULAR SAYING...

"IT'S HARD TO LISTEN TO REALITY SOMETIMES. FICTION HAS DONE SO MUCH MORE TO RAISE ME."

AS I GREW, THERE WAS A SWORD OF DAMOCLES OVER ME.

I FELT I NEEDED AN ADVENTURE.

OR I'D **NEVER** GROW UP.

HA! YOUR FEMALE VALUE IS SLIPPING AWAY!

POR QUÉ?!

SO, FRIDAY NIGHT?

I LIKE YOU, BUT...

IT MADE DATING A **NIGHTMARE**.

AS I GREW OLDER AND CONSUMED MORE FICTION, THE STORY WAS THE **SAME**.

EXPIRATION WAS IMPENDING.

AND THEN I FOUND JANE EYRE.

FROM HERE OUT THERE BE SPOILERS, YO.

FOR A GOTHIC ROMANCE, IT BEGINS UNROMANTICALLY.

JANE IS "PLAIN, OBSCURE, POOR, AND LITTLE."

IT WAS THE FIRST TIME I'D READ A NOVEL WITH A "NORMAL" HEROINE.

THE ROMANCE DOESN'T HAVE TYPICAL NARRATIVE PACING.

THE WEDDING OCCURS MIDWAY THROUGH THE BOOK.

THE BUILD-UP TO THE WEDDING IS SO OMINOUS.

GIVEN MY FEARS, THIS WAS A PERFECT HOOK FOR ME.

FICTIONAL RELATIONSHIPS ARE OFTEN BUILT ON SHAKY FOUNDATIONS.

IT WAS THE FIRST TIME I'D SEEN A STORY THAT SAID...

STOP! THIS MAN IS MARRIED ALREADY!

"YOU CAN LOVE SOMEONE AND NOT LOSE YOURSELF."

"SOMETIMES, YOU MUST GO."

YES, IT CAN HURT TO DEVIATE FROM THE SCRIPT. IT CAN LEAVE YOU FRIENDLESS OR DESTROY YOU.

BUT IF YOU ARE STEADFAST...

...YOU CAN MAKE YOURSELF A RICH LIFE.

YOU CAN CREATE MEANINGFUL NON-ROMANTIC RELATIONSHIPS.

AND IF YOU **WANT** A ROMANTIC RELATIONSHIP...

...YOU CAN ALSO HAVE THAT.

BUT YOU CAN HAVE IT ON YOUR OWN TERMS.

THE BOOK **DOES END** IN MARRIAGE.

BUT EVEN THAT SEEMED TAILOR MADE FOR ME.

IT'S NOT THE LAST THING TO HAPPEN IN JANE'S LIFE.

AT THE END, JANE IS TELLING US HER STORY TEN YEARS AFTER SHE'S MARRIED.

SO MAYBE IT WOULDN'T BE THE LAST THING TO HAPPEN IN MY LIFE.

SO, ARE YOU **FREE** TONIGHT?

MAYBE IT WAS JUST A THING TO BE ENJOYED, NOT DEFINED BY.

JANE EYRE BROUGHT SO MUCH TO MY LIFE. IT'S FLAWED, BUT IT CHALLENGED SOME OF MY MOST TOXIC EARLY IDEAS. SO I'LL LET BRONTË HERSELF CLOSE THIS OUT.

"I remembered that the real world was wide, and that a varied field of hopes and fears, of sensations and excitements, awaited those who had the courage to go forth into its expanse, to seek real knowledge of life amidst its perils."

-Charlotte Brontë, Jane Eyre

A Different Kind of Fantasy Roleplay

Brandy Dawley, illustration by Leslie Doyle

You come to a door.

Some doors should not be opened, but you are an adventurer, and seasoned adventurers never leave doors unopened, no matter what might be hiding behind them.

Every adventure starts with opening a door to something. Something daunting. Something terrifying. Something with potential to drop riches beyond your wildest imagining. Dragons. Goblins. Or worse... Boys. You open the door.

You walk into the dark room. The only light is on a lonely table. In the room, there sits a lone adventurer. He is handsome. Hair the color of pilfered gold coins, eyes that look like they were crafted from the jewel horde of a High Dragon, and a mouth that could heal wounds. You can tell he's a rogue before you see his weaponry – from the glint in his eye, from the dangerous way the corners of his mouth curl at the sides, from the shiver that runs up your back when his gaze catches yours.

You're a mixed-class chaotic neutral homebrew character who put all her points into CHA. You are unarmed, except for Weaponized Cuteness, a few spells, and a +5 Smile of Disarming.

You approach him.

Roll for initiative.

High roll. Take your turn.

ADVENTURER
WANTED

Singles Night ♥
LADIES
NO COVER

You approach him. You speak. "Are you looking for a group, or should I just battle you and steal your loot?"

He grins and you feel the tendrils of a familiar spell wrapping around you, as you realize you aren't the only one who has Weaponized Cuteness locked down. Finally you've met someone playing at the same level as you. You just hope you don't fumble your roll. "That depends," he says, "on what kind of loot you're looking for. I have a pretty rare wand with +7 durability, so I guess the question is, are you high enough level to wield it?"

That sounds like valuable loot.

Roll Charisma check.

Natural 20. He looks at you. He clearly likes what he sees. He bites his lip and offers you a seat. "I could use an adventuring party"

"Good," you reply. "I've been looking for a companion to venture into the Cavern of Secrets, and things might get hard."

"Oh," he says, "things are definitely getting hard."

Yep, you want that wand.

His eyes catch yours. You see the mirth in his eyes as he gazes intently into you. He's casting another spell. For a rogue, he has a dangerous amount of magic at his disposal. Probably another multiclass homebrew character. Multiclass homebrew characters can be such monsters, sometimes.

Roll Fortitude.

You fumble. You're Dickmatized, for five rounds, unable to look away, and you feel your heart pounding.

"I'd be careful venturing into the Cavern of Secrets," you say. "You'll drown if you're not careful."

He laughs. "The wetter the better. I've got gills."

Gills, high charisma, that wand, and a seemingly endless set of spells. Not only is he rolling natural 20s in this conversation, he is rolling natural 20s in life. There's something damnably smug about him, something familiar. Suddenly, you know who he is. The creature sitting in front of you is the stuff of lore, the subject of stories whispered breathlessly by tavern maids.

"I've heard of your legendary wand. +6 to Storm Damage, as I recall. And me without a tarp in my adventurer's pack." You wink at him.

"You'll find your quests a breeze if you keep using your Flattery spell," he tells you.

"It's just a cantrip," you reply, "I have an unlimited supply. I'm just power leveling to keep up with you."

"I hope you like explosions," he says, "and you might want to stock up on Greater Stamina potions. I feel like they might come in handy."

"You'd better go into that cave with that big sword of yours drawn," you say.

He shakes his head. "A real warrior goes *head first* into danger," he says, winking and running his tongue over those wicked lips of his, and the look in his eyes underlines the meaning of his words.

Right. He mentioned he had gills.

BAM. A disembodied voice in your head yells gleefully, "+150 XP TO THE ROGUE!"

Suddenly, a gust of wind comes through the room. The lights are blown out. It is pitch dark. You feel his breath against your neck.

Roll Perception check.

Your perception check fails miserably. You have no idea where this might go. There's something about him that gets under your skin, but you can't tell if it's a pleasant itch or an irritant. You don't know if he's a trustworthy ally, or if you've met a dragon in disguise.

You have two choices now. You can stay here for the night as his companion, or you can use the darkness as your advantage, attack him, loot him, walk out of the room, and start out on your adventure alone. But before you make your decision, remember your alignment. Your alignment determines your actions, always.

Roll for initiative.

WE MET ON A QUEST TO DESTROY ATHEON.

NERD LOVE
BY IRENE KOH

2 MONTHS LATER, WE MET IN CALIFORNIA. IN ANOTHER 3, SHE MOVED IN WITH ME.

LIFE WAS PERFECT.

I COULD BE MY NERDY SELF AROUND HER.

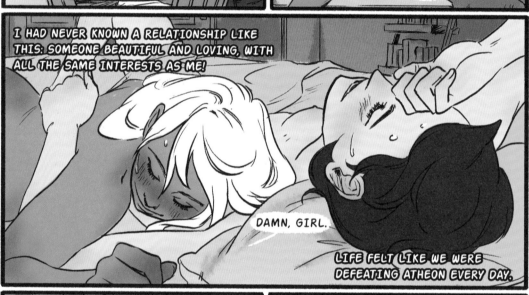

Giant-Sized Regrets

Jess Oliver-Proulx

I hadn't really noticed Jack. Not right away. He had just been the guy in the kitchen who had perfected my order. Turkey club sandwich with caesar dressing instead of mayo, he always remembered. Jack and I had been coworkers for a couple of months and I didn't know too much about him. Stalkbook wouldn't be a thing for another four or five years. What I knew about Jack I had learned from in-person interactions. Like we did back in the day. When things were cool.

When Jack wasn't slaving behind the grill in the kitchen he bussed tables. Moving between the crowds, 50 pounds of pint glasses and flat beer in a bus bin hovering above his head. When the day was slow, he'd belt out ballads from Alice in Chains or Pearl Jam into a kitchen spatula. He read graphic novels and played an old GameBoy on his breaks. Once a week after work, he and several other co-workers had a *Dungeons & Dragons* session after close.

Before Jack, I hadn't known many "geeky" people simply because I moved around too much. I was never in any place long enough to really make friends. In high school I tried to make nice with the MTG guys that played in the hall but they mostly seemed confused and slightly annoyed that I was talking to them. Needless to say, I did not play Magic: The Gathering.

As a kid, my fandom was expressed "subtly." I sketched Bat signals and *Mortal Kombat* dragons all over my school books and World Famous messenger bag. While my girlfriends were getting french manicures for our 8th-grade graduation, I had white Batman symbols airbrushed on my nails. The day after graduation I went back to the nail salon, changed the bats to black and added green Riddler question marks. It was 1995, Joel Schumacher was shitting all over Batman, but my nails looked fierce.

One day in the staff room before our shift started, Bradley, a fellow server/my BFF, overheard one of Jack's phone conversations. Jack had mentioned that he was interested in the new girl (me) but didn't think I would go out with him so he wasn't going to ask.

I was floored. "Really? Jack?" I could feel a rose flush over my cheeks. I had always thought he was attractive but never entertained the idea of asking him on a date. My hands started to sweat.

Until then, I hadn't had a lot of success with the opposite sex. I was the tomboy who my crushes never noticed. *Tekken Tag* partner? Yes. Romantic interest? Not a chance. The guys I was into never reciprocated. But this. This was different. Alien territory. I didn't know how to flirt. What was that? Is there a book for this? Flashes of Monica accidentally cutting off Chandler's toe in her failed flirting fiasco whirled around my brain. I'm gonna cock this up. I know it.

Jack was a few years older than I was and I didn't really know how to break the ice. It never occurred to me that I could open with a simple 'Hello.' No way. What kind of weirdo just says 'Hi' without a plan?

I was overthinking it. After all, I knew he already kinda liked me. It should have been simple.

However, having suffered serious rejection in the past, I wanted to minimize the possibility of that happening again.

I asked Bradley how he would break the ice. I wanted to be as smooth as possible.

"I have an old comic book that might do the trick," Bradley replied.

I looked at him suspiciously, "Is it called 'The Monkey's Paw' because I don't think I'm down with that."

"No" he laughed. It's the first appearance of Wolverine in *Giant Size X-Men* #1. Jack is a massive fanboy, he'll love it."

"That sounds kind of rare, are you sure you want to part with that?"

"It might be. You know I don't know comics. Truthfully, if Jack was gay I would have used this to seduce him already."

I chuckled. "Where did you even get this book?"

"My ex-boy left it after I kicked him out for cheating."

"Can I at least pay you for it?"

"Nope. Keep your money. Knowing I gave it away for free is all the payment I need, honey."

A few weeks later, I acquired this Legendary Comic Book of Ice Breaking from Bradley the Wingman.

After reading the book (because of course I read it, it's Wolverine!), I calculated the perfect moment to "casually" give the gift to Jack.

"You're going to see *X-Men* this weekend, right?" I asked Jack after work one Wednesday.

"Oh hell yes, I have midnight screening tickets! I've been waiting my whole life for this. The kid in me is freaking out."

This was it. My window. Be smooth.

"I also have midnight tickets, maybe I'll see you there?" I totally lied.

"Yes! Sit with us!" Jack replied. "I'll save you a seat!"

I was in. Now all I had to do was show up with the comic book. And you know, get a ticket to the midnight screening.

Thursday we arranged to meet at the movie theater at 11 pm. Even though we arrived an hour early, our group was unable to sit together so we paired up and sat where we could. Jack grabbed my hand and darted for the first set of seats he could find that were not in the front row.

As we settled in and waited for the film to start, I pulled the comic from my purse and handed it to him.

"Oh, by the way..." I started, "I've had this book kicking around my house for a while but I don't really collect comics. I feel like it should go to someone who would really appreciate it."

Jack paused for what seemed like an eternity. He stared at the book, jaw slung open, unable to speak.

He didn't even want to touch the plastic.

"Are... are you giving this to me?" He asked in disbelief. As if I had just handed him The Ring.

"Yes."

"No. Are you sure? Do you know what this is? No. I can't. Seriously?"

"Yes," I smirked with +5 charisma.

Jack sat back in his seat. "This is beyond generous and the nicest thing anyone has ever done."

I laughed. "Well, you know, you do make a pretty sweet club. Call it even?" He smiled.

As the lights began to dim and the film started to roll, Jack grabbed my hand and squeezed tight. My stomach fluttered so intensely I thought I was going to throw up. If it wasn't for the opening scene I probably would have. At the end of the night, Jack gave me a bear hug and kissed both my hands as we parted ways. I was crushing hard and I hoped he knew it by now.

Over the next few months, Jack courted me from the kitchen via adorable edible messages on my plate, spatula serenades, and napkin flowers, but he never asked me out on a date. Jack had game, but it was long.

It was now Halloween weekend. Jack arrived for his busser shift rocking an impressive Wolverine costume complete with natural chops that he'd been growing out for months.

When he laid eyes on my costume he dropped his bus bin.

I was Storm.

After he finished gushing, during the rest of the shift I could feel his gaze. Every time I looked at him he was already looking back.

Before the end of the evening, he grabbed my hand and led me to the dance floor.

"You should take your break right now," he said, "There is no way I'm letting this evening go by without dancing with Storm."

'Never Tear Us Apart' began to play and he pulled me close, holding me tight against his chest. I could feel his heart pounding erratically. Knowing he was nervous made me feel less so. Had we not been in the middle of a shift and in front of the entire staff, I would have gone in for the kiss.

At the end of the song he looked me in the eyes but, didn't say anything at first. As if he was still unsure that I would say yes if he asked. He kissed my hands, thanked me for the dance and we went back to work.

At the end of the evening after our shift was over and the bar was closed, Jack finally asked me out on a real date.

It turns out, when you wait that long and build up someone in your head, they rarely live up to the fantasy.

The reality is, I should have gotten to know him more before presenting him with such a rare and exquisite gift. The lesson I learned that day was this: partners will come and go, but vintage comics are forever.

Puzzled Over Pints

♫DOOT DEET DOOT♫

JEN! WHAT'S UP?

DIDJAWANNAGAMEWITH MESONIA?!

HELL YES! CAN I BRING JAMES?

SEE YOU AROUND SEVEN AT CAFE MOX!

SO HEED THIS WARNING, SIGNIFICANT OTHERS CAN GAME WITH YOU BUT MAKE SURE YOU HAVE A DEDICATED GAMING GROUP. YOUR FRIENDS ARE YOUR MANA POOL. TAP THEM.

NEVER THE END

4 Fictional Happy Endings

(That Are About To Go Tragically Wrong)

Diana McCallum

Watch any movie with a romantic storyline and you'll likely be bombarded with the theme that love conquers all, fate will bring people together and couples always get a happy ending. If you happen to be festering in a dating slump at the time you may also find yourself screaming, "Why not me?!?" at the television while downing a litre of Häagen-Dazs and scrolling through slash fanfiction on your phone. Well, good news, it turns out you're better off not being one of those fictional couples, because after the credits rolled a lot of the folks that seemed to get a happy ending were actually royally screwed, some quite literally. For example…

4. Westley and Buttercup Will Be Murdered. Soon.
(*The Princess Bride*)

I shouldn't have to tell you the plot of *The Princess Bride*, but in case you've spent your life on a deserted island with only this book for comfort I wouldn't want you to be confused (and I also totally understand if you need to burn this book for kindling to stay warm, no hard feelings). So, the story goes, Westley and Buttercup fall in love. Westley leaves to find some sweet ocean money. Buttercup gets engaged to an evil Prince who tries to kill her so he can start a war. Westley saves her, is mostly killed, then saves her again, decides not to kill the evil Prince and then Westley and Buttercup ride off into the sunset together.

It's a classic (albeit roundabout) love story, but what you probably didn't know about *The Princess Bride* is that Westley and Buttercup are going to be murdered in about…immediately after the credits.

How you ask? Well, let's list what we know about evil Prince Humperdink: he's got a name even a mother couldn't love and his hobbies include hunting and going to war. And he loves those two hobbies. He has Buttercup kidnapped so he can frame the neighbouring country for her death, and then easily hunted down Westley and Buttercup. Now jump to the film's climax where we have Westley and Buttercup tying Humperdink up, in his own castle, while still completely conscious, and then escaping by diving out the bedroom window *without even gagging him*! Are you freaking kidding me? That dude is going to bellow his whiny ass off the second they're gone, which means there will be guards in that room faster than you can say inconceivable, and a whole army on the lovers' trail not long after that. An army that earlier that day was getting ready to go to war so will be fully prepared for a late-night murder binge in the countryside.

Which puts a new perspective on that beautiful kiss Westley and Buttercup share on a hilltop at the very end. That's a good-bye kiss because there is definitely a legion of soldiers about to come up there and slaughter them on Prince Humperdink's order. But a solid kiss, nonetheless.

3. Jocelyn Is Still Marrying Adhemar (*A Knight's Tale*)

A Knight's Tale is the story of Heath Ledger as a peasant named William Thatcher who is hella good at jousting so he lies about being a knight so he can enter competitions. During this charade he also falls in love with a woman named Jocelyn (yay!) and gains a mortal enemy named Count Adhemar (boo!), so it's an up and down few months for William.

Near the end of the movie William is arrested for impersonating a knight just before the big tournament and Adhemar arranges to marry

Jocelyn against her will, because the 14th century wasn't exactly huge on women's lib yet.

But then we get to the big finale where William gets pardoned by Prince Edward, makes it to the tournament and absolutely destroys Adhemar in the final joust. The peasants rejoice and William and Jocelyn embrace with excitement.

And that's all well and good, except *there was never an agreement that the winner of the tournament gets to marry Jocelyn.* Adhemar made a private arrangement with Jocelyn's father that he would get to marry her, because he's a rich Count and can do that, and then the tournament was just this other thing that was also happening the same day. So even though Adhemar lost the joust he's still scheduled to marry Jocelyn, which makes this ending *absolutely terrifying.*

Throughout the movie Adhemar is shown to be petty and violent, and now that William has embarrassed him in front of the entire kingdom you can be damn sure he's going to make a spectacle of marrying Jocelyn as revenge, treating her like shit and making sure she never sees William again, which wouldn't be hard because, again, 14th century women's lib was pretty bare bones.

So Adhemar is definitely going to take Jocelyn away from William forever, but what he can't take away is how good William is at knocking men off horses with a stick. Super good stick poking bro, well done. Which leads us to the moral of the story; true love conquers literally nothing because the 14th century suuuuuuuuuuucked.

2. Every Disney Marriage (Every Disney Movie)

You may want to make yourself some calming chamomile tea because I'm about to hit you with a shocking statistic: the average age of a Disney princess is 14-16 years old.

That's right, the majority of Disney princesses get married before they're legally allowed to drive and yet we're raised to believe the dudes they met and married in the same day will be their life long companions and everything will be hunky-dory forever. Bullshit. These are teenage girls impulsively devoting their lives to absolute strangers and relationships that can only end in disaster. But don't take my vague word on it, let's run through some specifics.

Belle is a seventeen year old girl when she marries The Beast, a relationship more likely fuelled by Stockholm Syndrome than it is love. And if you're thinking, yeah, Beast held Belle prisoner in his castle but he was also a real sweet guy, then I've got news for you. The Beast was a royally manipulative douche the whole time. For example, one of Beast's 'romantic gestures' is to give Belle a library of books after one of their dates. Belle's response is to thank him for being so generous that he would extend her prison to the entire house now that she had been there for a few weeks. But there was literally nothing generous about the act of giving the library to her. The books were already in the house, by not letting her have access to them until she had been there for awhile Beast successfully manipulated Belle into thinking he was a super great guy. One visit to a shrink after they get married and Belle's going to realize that what she thinks is love is really just a deep-seated survival mechanism and she needs to get the heck out of there with an apron stuffed full of non-sentient silverware.

And then there's Ariel who at sixteen years old married literally the first human being she ever interacted with. Even ignoring that their personalities might clash because they've barely spoken, how are their cultures possibly compatible? Every friend and family member Ariel has lives in the ocean, and Prince Eric rules over a coastal kingdom whose main resource is undoubtedly fishing. Congratulations Ariel, your new husband and his subjects make their living by hunting and eating your friends. That won't be a horrifying thing to learn when she opens her wedding reception meal to find her best friend, Flounder, on her plate, mouthing, "Why Ariel? I thought you loved me!"

And don't forget fourteen year old Snow White and her handsome prince that she's literally never spoken to, who... you know what guys, I can't lie, if he can keep from kissing corpses on a regular basis I think those crazy kids just might make it work.

1. Christian's Going To Die Just Like Satine (*Moulin Rouge*)

Admittedly, *Moulin Rouge* doesn't have the happiest of endings. Satine dies and the Moulin Rouge is shut down but the love story between Satine and Christian is still beautiful, as they uphold the ideals of the bohemian revolutionaries by telling The Duke to stick it.

Satine dying right after they reconcile is kind of sad, but if it makes you feel better please know that Christian will be joining her in death very, very soon.

You see Satine died of "consumption", a fun old-timey word for tuberculosis, a disease that is pretty infectious if you live with someone who has it, especially if they cough or laugh a lot to spread the disease through the air. None of the medical journals consulted mentioned how singing affects the spread of tuberculosis, but it's a safe bet that pushing air out of your body and trying to project it as far as possible probably falls under the category of, Oh God You're Making It So Much Worse.

Satine was at her most contagious just before death and Christian was making out and sleeping with her as often as possible, which means his lungs are now a tuberculosis feeding ground. The disease can take a few years to kill you though, so Christian probably has enough time to publish his novel before he takes the old dirt nap with his one true love who accidentally took him down with her.

This movie says the greatest thing you'll ever learn is just to love and be loved in return. I say the greatest thing you'll ever learn is the need to tell your partner you have an infectious disease that could kill them, but maybe that's why I don't write musicals.

Ménage à 3

☙❧

Gisèle Lagacé & David Lumsdon with colours by Shouri

I read a lot of comics growing up. I even kept reading them in my early twenties while on the road, touring with my all-girl band. Now that I'm older, and STILL reading them, it's safe to say comics and music hold a very important place in my life. If I'm not doing music, I'm doing comics, and vice versa. When the time came for Dave and me to give rocker chick Zii a job in *Ménage à 3*, it only felt natural to have her find one in a comic shop. Plus, we knew from the start of the series that she read comics growing up. Once Zii discovered all the perks from working in a comic shop, we knew she'd go to great lengths to get the job! I can hear you now: "Is Zii you?" No, she's not. Okay... maybe a little bit. Write what you know, right?

– Gisèle Lagacé, artist and co-writer on Ma3comic.com

A comic book store?!

Yes! You'd be what's known as "counter candy."

Oo, moi j'aime the candy!

Indie chicks are a plus at comic book stores 'cause comic book geeks think they have a shot with them. This increases visits *and* revenue. It's how the business *survives!*

Okay, and what makes you think they'll hire me just like that?

Junghan works here. He'll hook you up. Right, Jung?

Oh... heheh... hi, Jung. How's the eye?

171

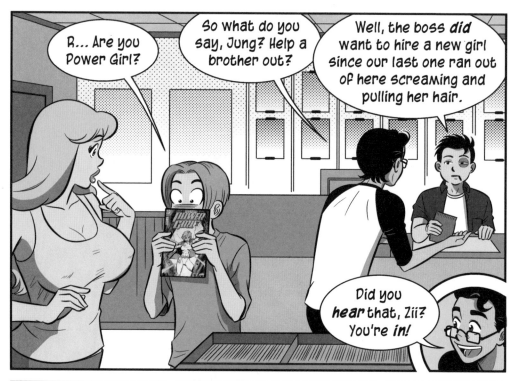

R... Are you Power Girl?

So what do you say, Jung? Help a brother out?

Well, the boss *did* want to hire a new girl since our last one ran out of here screaming and pulling her hair.

Did you *hear* that, Zii? You're *in!*

Zii? Where'd you...

...go.

BD ADULTE | HENTAI | YAOI

Ee hee hee heeeeee

I'd get discounts, right?

Not so fast! Before she's hired, she must sell one of...

xie trix comix

POWER PACHYDERMS

...THESE!

⋛Gasp⋜ Not **Power Pachyderms #1?!** That's the most **vile** comic in **creation!**

Power Whozits?

Summer '89... Marvel tried to recreate the X-men as ⋛shudder⋜ **anthropomorphic talking elephants!** My **eyes,** they **burn!!!**

That's right! We can't even **give** these away!

Sell an issue and you're hired. It's how we test prospects.

Cakewalk!

Hey, Poindexter. Buy all of these, and I'll kiss Blondie here.

Zii!!!

You want me to get the job, don't you?

174

Sticky Dilly Buns

Gisèle Lagacé & Shouri

Anyone who knows me, knows I'm not repressed when it comes to sex. I joke about it all the time, so much so that it's reflected in the comics I work on. It's also very important to me that it's shown in a positive way. I want to help people be more open about sex, and understanding of others too. Sexually repressed Ruby in *Sticky Dilly Buns* is the perfect character for such a task. Shouri and I had her move in with her ex-porn star sister, Amber, and super-mega-gay Dillon. That is BOUND to affect someone, right? Especially if that someone somehow gets into her roommate's boy's love manga collection, and then somehow ends up at a comic shop looking for more 'cause, you know, maybe said roommate would want more books added to his collection? That yaoi would NEVER be FOR that someone! Oh no – noooo!

– Gisèle Lagacé, co-artist/writer on StickyDillyBuns.com

Well, now that that's taken care of, I really need to get to work.

So do I. Busy day ahead!

Yeah... uhm... me too...

I know, right? We work hard for our money!

Bye, Ruby!

SLAM

...

Guess I really need to find a job.

Can't spend my day reading that... that *yaoi!*

I need to get out there! Explore my options!

Well, you never *know.* They *could* be hiring someone with a B.B.A.

Minew!

And with a cat in her bag. Yeah, totally!

Yaoi

Minew!

More like "meow!" Have you *seen* this couple? They're so hot and--

What am I saying?!

What am I *doing?!*

Minew!

Oh God... what kind of perverted degenerate have I turned into?

Yaoi

I have to stop before it's too late. Before I'm caught! Dillon's already on to me!

If anyone else found out, I could just kiss respectability goodb--

Little Ruby Larose? Is that you?

All right, you've caught me. Laugh all you want now!

Caught you? Laugh? Ruby... why would I laugh?

Because now you *know!*

Yeahhh... I... know what you look like. You've grown into a very fine young woman!

Oh. That. Uhhh. Yes! I did.

So what brings you into a comic shop?

This is a comic shop? No *wonder* I couldn't find *real* books!

Not a fan of graphic novels?

Books shouldn't have pictures!

It's too bad. We have a really good sale on yaoi; buy two, get one free.

Glbzt!

Okay, maybe I should laugh a *little.*

A s-s-sale on ya-yaoi?

New releases included!

R-r-really?

If you were a yaoi fan like me, you'd be all over this.

All the pretty pictures... they'rrre... heavenly.

Hh-hh-heav--

Well, not for you. You don't like books with pictures.

T-t-true, but one should always try new things. Ha-ha!

That's what I like to hear! To start, I recom--

Volumes 3, 4 & 5 of this deliciously naughty series...?

...What about volumes 1 & 2?

Well, I, I like to start *in medias res*, you know, just to make it a little more intellectually chall--

She bought them yesterday.

GHOST STORIES

ANNIE MOK

"Let me stand aside, to see the phantoms of those days go by me, accompanying the shadow of myself, in dim procession."
— CHARLES DICKENS, David Copperfield

I was eight in 1995 when the Casper movie came out.

I SAW IT, BOUGHT THE NOVELIZATION, MADE "CASPER" MY PASSWORD FOR A.O.L., AND GOT GOT YELLED AT BY MY MOM FOR READING A NOVELIZATION.

I FIXATED ON CASPER AND HIS ACHE FOR
CONNECTION. (HE'S A GHOST)

AT THE CLIMAX, THE ANGEL-SPIRIT OF CASPER'S
DEAD MOM TURNS HIM INTO A "REAL BOY"
TIL TEN, "LIKE CINDARELLA," SO HE CAN
DANCE WITH HIS CRUSH, THE LIVING (AND
THUS IMPOSSIBLE TO TOUCH) CHRISTINA RICCI.

TEEN DREAMBOAT DEVON SAWA PLAYED
THE "REAL BOY" CASPER. I DIDN'T KNOW
THAT I WASN'T A BOY, DIDN'T KNOW
THAT I LIKED BOYS.

IN 1996, I FOUND A NEW SERIES AT THE SCHOLASTIC BOOK FAIR, WHICH SET UP A AS A LITTLE SHOP IN THE HALLWAY OF W.W.-P. UPPER ELEMENTARY SCHOOL A COUPLE OF TIMES A YEAR.

ONE OF the <u>ANIMORPHS</u> COVERS FEATURED A DREAMY BOY TURNING INTO A HAWK.

TOBIAS, THAT BOY, TURNED OUT TO BE A BABY JAMES DEAN-STYLE LONER WITH NO PARENTS.

TOBIAS ACCIDENTALLY GOT TRAPPED IN HIS "MORPH," STUCK IN THE BODY OF A RED-TAILED HAWK. HE COMMUNICATED WITH the 4 OTHER TEENS ON the TEAM THRU SPEECH-LIKE TELEPATHY. HE DEVELOPED A STAR-CROSSED RELATIONSHIP WITH RACHEL, the TOUGH TOMBOY OF the TEAM.

THEY LOOKED FOR WAYS to STOP the ONGOING INVASION OF YEERKS, SLUG-LIKE ALIENS THAT WRAPPED AROUND PEOPLE'S BRAINS AND CONTROLLED THEIR MINDS.

WE GO to the MOVIES and READ BOOKS
to DREAM AWAKE.

AN ALIEN SLUG IN the BRAIN — I COULD
UNDERSTAND THAT. I COULDN'T ALLOW
MYSELF to SAY HOW VIOLATED I FELT
BY MY MOM, HOW I FELT SHE
INHABITED ME.

A CUTE C.G.I. CARTOON GHOST BOY
STOOD IN FOR ME, AND HOW I SAT
OUTSIDE MY DISTANT BODY.

There's Nothing Wrong, It Must Be Love

Diana McCallum

When I was twenty years old I got my first super serious boyfriend. I had been dating since high school but had never been with anyone for more than a few weeks so it was exciting to be smitten for the first time in my life.

And this guy had everything. He was cute, funny, awkwardly charming, he respected me, made me laugh, and we were both giant nerds. We chatted on MSN Messenger the day after we met and I asked what he was doing. He said he was watching *Stargate*. I felt my heart flutter. He was perfect.

We'd been dating for a month when he told me that he loved me. I didn't feel the same yet so I told him I was falling in love with him. A month later I told him I loved him too and really thought that I meant it.

After a year and a half of dating we moved in together and learned each other's quirks, like how he was scared of germs but hated to clean, and how I was too cheerful in the mornings for a sane person to handle.

But it was manageable stuff. Nothing monstrous. Just the regular things you learn about people when you live together. Things remained perfect.

He got a job as a middle school teacher. I started work as a legal secretary. We got a dog. We had supper with his parents every Sunday and watched superhero cartoons every night before bed. As I said, life was perfect.

Except every now and then a dark thought would creep into my mind. I wasn't sure if this was love.

We made each other laugh, had great conversations, we never fought, we had the same interests, we supported each other. There was nothing else I could think of that I could want in a life mate so I'd tell myself this *must* be love, and my mouth would say the words, but still, I wasn't sure.

I was so unsure, I would spend hours at my kitchen table weighing the pros and cons of our relationship, with the con side coming out at practically zero every time. There was nothing wrong so I'd tell myself this *must* be love.

Then one day my mother took me dress shopping. I can't remember what the event was, but the shopping trip itself turned into one of the most important days of my life. I tried on a red and white dress and told my mother I liked it.

"Put it back then," she said, "we'll find something you love."

And that was the end of the conversation because this was the woman who knew me best in the entire world. She knew that I was capable of loving something with all my heart and wouldn't let me settle for a dress that I just liked. Half an hour later we found a black and white flower dress that I loved so much I still wear it to this day.

When I got home I couldn't stop thinking about what my mom had said because she was completely right. I was capable of loving things passionately. I was a nerd, loving things passionately was what I did! I had an obsession with Batman and Robin since I was eight. I devoted hundreds of hours to writing fanfiction. I went to a *Lord of the Rings* Extended Version marathon dressed as an elf. Of course I could love passionately. And the sad truth I had to face was that I loved my new dress more deeply than I loved my boyfriend.

Some would say the spark had gone out of our relationship, but I was starting to realize it had never been lit at all. I was with someone that I cared for but didn't love the way I needed to love someone I would spend my life with. Once I accepted this I had the bigger problem of figuring out what to do with this epiphany. I was twenty-two years old, in the first real relationship of my life and faced with a scenario I had never dreamed of.

Could I really leave this amazing guy and the picture perfect life we had built on the off chance that I would eventually find someone I felt more passionately about? Could I upend both of our lives on the possibility of finding something that was just a little bit more? It sounded crazy to even consider it. I thought about my boyfriend and how leaving would shatter him to his core. I thought about my friends and family and how they all said we were an amazing couple. They would be disappointed in me. They'd hate me for not appreciating what I had, for throwing it away. So I didn't. I stayed. And generally I was happy. That's the rub.

Then something truly terrible happened. A friend of mine was killed in a car accident. I hadn't talked to him in months but we had been close once. He had taken me to prom. My friend was amazing. He wrote biting poetry and played in a band and went to school abroad and travelled all over the world. My friend experienced life in every form he could in the short twenty-three years he had on this earth and I was devastated thinking about the potential the world had been robbed of and all the things he would have done. And I thought he would be disappointed in me that I was staying somewhere that didn't fulfill me.

I was approaching three years with my boyfriend. When we would visit his parents they would subtly mention grandchildren. Meanwhile I knew in my heart if he asked me to marry him, I would say no. I had to end things. I absolutely had to. I had wasted years of both of our lives, but I couldn't let us waste any more time.

Except I could. I waited three more months. It took me that long to gather the courage to sit him down and end things, and it was the hardest thing I've ever done in my life. I was physically shaking as I told a man who had supported me, laughed with me, and possibly truly loved me, that I also loved him, but not in the way I needed. I loved him as a friend, as a confidante, but not passionately, not like someone I could spend my life with. He was devastated, but I don't think completely surprised. He asked me if there was someone else. There wasn't, but I think it might have been easier if there had been. If I had been leaving him for another man that would have been tangible, that would have been a reason. Instead I was abandoning this perfect life for the potential of meeting someone else, someone I might not ever find. I think that was maddening to him. It was frustrating for me too. But it was done. We parted as amicably as possible. Our friends were confused, our families were disappointed, I'm not sure he knew what to feel.

As for me, I felt free. I regretted hurting him but knew in my heart I had finally done the right thing. And now I was truly excited about life for the first time in years.

The first thing I did was move to a new city. I needed a drastic change. A few months after that I moved again because the change had been too drastic. I dated a few boys along the way. They were mostly lovely and treated me well, but none of them lit a fire in me.

I had been single for two years when I turned to online dating and algorithms and search boxes. I found a cute boy from Newfoundland who mentioned Batman in his profile seven times. We met for a coffee and I finally knew what love felt like.

When I look back on my earlier relationship I feel like a fool for convincing myself that what I had back then was love. The fact that I questioned it at all, and so constantly, should have proven that it wasn't. I'm embarrassed it took me as long as it did to end things, but I honestly have no regrets because that exact sequence of events brought me to where I am today.

I love the man I'm with now, I'm as certain about that as I am that Tim Drake is the best Robin. He supports me but respects my independence. He makes me laugh but he also challenges me. He pushes me to be better, to work harder, to think bigger, and even after three and a half years together I feel my chest tighten with excitement when he walks in the room. He's every feeling I was missing in my life for all those years.

I guess what I learned is that my mom was right (as moms often are), I'm capable of loving passionately and I believe anyone who identifies as a nerd or a geek is as well. So if that's you, please don't settle in life. Be with someone who makes you feel as excited as a new *Star Wars* trailer. There's a partner out there for you somewhere that you can love as much as your passions. So love with all your heart. Love passionately. And don't stop looking because you think you've found love, stop when you absolutely know it.

Girls With Slingshots

Danielle Corsetto

When your circle of friends is comprised of a dominatrix librarian, a commitment-phobic drunk writer, a polyamorous florist and her girlfriend the asexual baker, your barista husband, your savvy deaf sister, her pirate boyfriend, and a kitten with permanent headgear, the uncommon tends to take over as the norm. In my now-concluded webcomic, *Girls With Slingshots*, being a nerd girl seems like a rarity.

But beloved geek girls are hardly rare in my own world, where every-other female friend of mine has inspired the cardigan-wearing, laptop-toting Maureen in some way, from their relentless love of *Star Trek*, to their love/hate relationship with a still-active LiveJournal account, or their neverending quest for a more addicting online game.

The story of Maureen "the Blog Girl" and Jameson "the Barista" begins with Friendster, evolves with awkward instant messaging dates, and ends (spoilers) in marital bliss. I'd be lying if I said that Maureen was easy for me to write; contrary to my profession as a cartoonist, I'm not much of a geek girl myself. But I've spent enough time at comic book conventions – and later with the friends I've made there – to be enchanted by the dynamic of the girl who geeks out over comic books, games, and programming, and the geeky and supportive husband who loves her.

In the last year alone, I've attended the dinosaur-and-pizza-themed wedding of my book-obsessed friends; the *Doctor Who*-themed wedding of my comic nerd friends; and the wedding of my cartoonist and computer geek friends whose cake was topped with Leia and Han figurines ("I love you." "I know.").

It's almost enough to make this commitment-phobic, sometimes-drunk writer want to be a beloved geek girl herself... almost. Honestly, I'd rather just write about her, because to me, she's a mystery wrapped in a cat GIF inside a custom-built gaming PC, and while I'll never fully understand her, I love seeing her in love.

I'm DOOMED, Jameson! My college savings are finally GONE.

Aw, sweetie... you know, it IS about time you got a job like the rest of us.

I know, honey, but.. but I'm SCARED!

Ah, baby. Scared of what? That you won't find anything good? That it won't pay enough? That you'll bomb the interview?

Scared that I'll have to leave my LAPTOP!

Ooh, no you don't. We'll start you on CRAIGSLIST.

PAT PAT

You haven't said anything about your ring.

Oh-- it's beautiful, but you know I don't know anything about jewelry.

Well, this particular ring is more than meets the eye.

What, does it morph into Optimus Prime?

Better. See that dark piece in the center of the stone? That's a tiny microchip which contains all of my passwords.

It's a symbol of my trust.

Does it have the password to your pants?

Yes, but it expires in ten seconds.

And now, the couple has written their own special vows for one another. Jameson?

Maureen... I promise you I'll always be as taken by you as I was the first time you messaged me on friendster...

...to comment on your blog posts when nobody else will, to provide for you only the fastest hi-speed internet, and only the finest brew of coffee for the rest of your days...

...and to always ask the waiter, "is there fish sauce in this?" before you order.

oOoh ♥ ♥ sweetie

By the power vested in me, I now pronounce you husband and wife.

You may now uh..

twitpic

OMG look we totally got hitched!!!

boodle♩ boot

1 TEXT from JAMESON

I'm so horny for you.

Hee hee. Really?

♫♪ YES. Are you coming home now?

TEXT TEXT TEXT

Getting in the car!

♫♪ I want you so bad.

text text

♫♪

Your gonna be up all night.

Well helloooo.

Did I use the wrong "your" again?

YES.

I'm so glad we're finally talking about this.

Sweetie, I've wanted to expand our family as well.

I'm not sure I can create one myself...

No one expects you to do that, silly! And there are older ones that need a good home, too.

Kitchen

You're right, Jameson, let's do it.

You wanna look at some tonight? I know a place that displays 'em right in the window.

Oooo pretty.

I guess they only come in white?

REFU

I kind of like our life the way it is.

Me too.

We get so much time alone together.

And yet, somehow, we can't get enough of each other.

sNXXkTzz

blog blog blog blog

Rise of the
Late Bloomer

Hope Nicholson, illustration by Kristen Gudsnuk

When I was a kid I loved *Choose Your Own Adventure* books, but I'd keep my finger in the pages before choosing the next step. Invariably, I'd end up with each finger stuck at a different path marker, so I could make sure that I picked the best ending.

When I read regular books, I would flip to the back and read the last three pages to make sure that I'd like the end before beginning the book.

I cheated at every videogame I ever played, just so I could get to the final end-scene quickly (which made playing *Chrono Trigger* with a dozen different endings, very frustrating!).

For the longest time I wished desperately I could do that with my life. I wanted to flip forward to the end of my story to find out the plot. Because I had a problem and I had no way of knowing the solution.

At 24 years old I was still a virgin and had never had a boyfriend.

I was torn between the desire to date ("It looks like so much fun on TV!") and undefined fear about it. If you asked me why I hadn't dated yet, I would have bolted out of the room. The frustration of not knowing why gave me intense anxiety, so I avoided thinking about it.

When I hung out with women, our talk would turn to romance, and feeling like a fraud, I would scramble to relate the very few experiences I had to their own actual love lives. I had a brief boyfriend at 17 where we mostly watched *Family Guy* and I let him lick my mouth while I tried not to show I was grossed out, a few unwelcome but unresisted physical advances by male friends that I had panic attacks over at 19 and 21, and a few chaste and unfulfilling dates here and there.

I ended up hanging out with gay men, and women who didn't date. I wonder now if these women were like me and were late bloomers, or whether they were just very discreet in their love affairs. Either way, I never heard about their romantic encounters and it made me feel more at ease. I avoided heterosexual men for years. I was scared of them, and I didn't know why.

Was I queer? I had a lot of crushes on men both real and fictional, but I never felt any similar type of obsession for women, so that seemed unlikely.

Was it body issues? Partly maybe, but after reading *Love & Rockets*, I felt assured that plump women could be hot.

Was I asexual? I hadn't been romantically involved with anyone, but the thought of being without sex for my entire life left me feeling panicked, not relieved.

I desired men. Yet, the thought of them being in the same room as me made my skin crawl. The thought of sitting across the room from a stranger no matter how attractive or likable made my stomach sink.

What the hell? That's not what *Sweet Valley High* told me romance would be like. Where was the man I would swoon over, who would occupy my every waking thoughts? The man who would graciously lose at *Mario Kart* and who would cuddle in bed with me on weekends while we read our favourite dog-eared comics?

At 24, I forced myself to play the game without a walkthrough. I made myself go on dates with strangers. I talked about pop culture and favourite foods, and wished that the whole thing was over five minutes in. Then I beat myself up for failing at this dating subquest.

I decided I couldn't figure this out on my own. So I went to a therapist. Who didn't help. I kept forcing myself to date. At one point I had a date where the seemingly impossible occurred, I was attracted to him! Then he promised to phone me and never contacted me again. That discouragement stopped me dating for another year.

I tried another therapist. This one was a better fit, but there was still no solution. These visits though were useful. They helped me verbalize my vague anxieties into actual words. Things are always scarier when they're giant formless clouds above your head.

One of my greatest fears was if I found a date I really liked, how I would tell them I was a virgin. I imagined them treating me with pity, or feeling fetishistic about being my first.

I was also scared to lose something that made me feel special. Being a virgin in a sexual world meant I had an anthropological viewpoint on society that I cherished. I knew all about sex, without ever having being touched. I felt it made me impartial and morally superior, more level-headed than people clouded with the fixations of love and sex.

I think I read too many books about unicorns only appearing to virgins.

Since talking in therapy seemed to help, I started talking more, to everyone. Friends. Strangers. Eventually, dates. The more I talked, the more comfortable I felt, the less overwhelming it seemed. My anxiety became manageable and I gained confidence. It became an oddball story, instead of a deeply seated fear. "Hello I'm Hope, I'm a 26-year-old virgin. No, I don't want to hire a prostitute to take care of it."

Eventually, I found a boy to kiss, in the most practical way possible, I went to a superhero make-out party (Toronto, am I right?). It went surprisingly well, but the subsequent dating failed spectacularly. You see, that brutal honesty I developed to cope with my anxiety? I demanded it returned in kind. If it wasn't, I transformed into a ball of judgmental fury (I was a virgin, but not a saint). I am still working on that to this day. But, it reassured me that physical affection was in fact, achievable for me. Days after the party, I tried kissing a fellow I had been awkwardly casually dating for four months. Again, miraculously, it went well! I had levelled up and achieved mutual physical attraction twice in a row. When it rains, it pours, and I was soaked. This romance also ended soon after, but we remain best friends to this day.

But this time, after being rejected, I didn't wait a year to recover. In RPGs when you get killed by a boss, you just need to keep grinding levels and upgrading equipment until you're strong enough to survive the battle. Every time I was rejected or dumped, it hurt. But it became less unusual, and I recovered quicker. I also realized that guys I was attracted to might be rare drops, but if I kept fighting, I found them.

I eventually fell into a romance with someone who didn't care at all that I was a virgin, and this indifference...was sort of hot. Oh, and he had the dreamiest eyes. We spent our first month together talking, playing videogames, and yeah, fooling around a bit. When we eventually had sex, it still felt scary, but it also felt right. And though this relationship didn't last long either, I don't regret it for a second.

I continue to be open about my late past. I didn't lose anything when I had sex, even my anthropological nature remained intact. Now, I'm awfully curious about other people and will listen raptly to anyone's love stories (which is why I created *Secret Loves of Geek Girls*!)

The amazing thing I discovered is that when I say I'm a late bloomer in a group, someone admits that they were, or are, one too.

I've been told this by men who admit I'm the second woman they've been with. I hear this from dates who tell me that they're not used to being told they're attractive. I've been told this by women who fear their boyfriends will pressure them into sex, and they don't know if they want it or not. I hear this from women who dated dozens of people for years with no emotional connection before finding someone who felt right. I hear this from women who fell in love with their partner a year into dating.

There is no walkthrough, because my path to feeling comfortable with dating wasn't theirs and it might not be yours either.

I've met so many virgins who are in their late twenties. Or those who lost their virginity young but regretted their first experience and avoided dating. They thought they were the only ones. They thought they'd have to have sex with someone they didn't feel comfortable with. They didn't know if they ever would like someone 'that way.' And I was relieved to hear that I wasn't alone or weird, that all of this is really normal variation, with no one set answer/reason to fit all of us. You might be queer, or asexual, or have to resolve past painful experiences. Or it might be that old adage of 'not having found the right fit.' Or for whatever social or biological reason, you are ready to date and be intimate at a much later age than society tells you is average.

It's awful that healing sometimes can happen only retroactively and not when you're struggling the most. I think if I had talked to any of these fellow late bloomers when I was a virgin, I wouldn't have felt as anxious. I'm hoping that by telling my story it will help some of you feel more confident about your life. And really, regardless of whether you have sex or not, that's the most important thing.

None the Wiser

A TRUE TALE OF LOVESICK FOOLISHNESS BY DIANA NOCK

WHY DID I THINK THIS WAS A GOOD IDEA?

WHAT WAS I TRYING TO ACCOMPLISH?

WHO DID I THINK I WAS FOOLING?

THIS WAS DOOMED FROM THE START.

ONE MONTH PREVIOUSLY

♪♪BRRR||||||||NNNGG♪♪BRRRR||||||

LIFE ISN'T A STORY. WELL, IT'S NOT JUST *MY* STORY, AT LEAST.

I CAN'T CONFUSE MY WISH FOR REALITY, AND I CAN'T TREAT OTHER PEOPLE LIKE CHARACTERS TO BE MANIPULATED TOWARD A SATISFYING RESOLUTION.

I HAVE *NO RIGHT*.

Heard It Through the Grapevine

Brandy Dawley

Straight talk, ladies. We have a problem. There's a big nasty chink in our armour and it's going to be the doom of us. You see, us girls, we've got a reputation. A pretty nasty one.

See, we're known for being catty. Competitive. More likely to get ahead by pulling another woman down than by building ourselves up. No matter how we try, no matter how many times we as a community band together to form a feminist-super-mecharobot, there's a big, ugly stain on our lady-positive badges we may never scrub out. Girl-on-girl hate is probably the only culturally reinforced trope bigger than… well…the OTHER girl-on-girl thing. It's a trope for a reason – from TV to movies to even comics, we're taught that the best way to get ahead is to pull each other down. Guys are taught to be better than other guys by striving to get ahead of them. Women are taught that, to be better than other ladies, we have to cut them down to our level. This is a critical exercise in stupidity, of course – because by pulling other women down, nobody gets ahead – all us ladies are still stuck wallowing in the muck of the trenches while meanwhile, dudes are pole-vaulting mountains. And there's a type of guy, he'll try to work that to his own advantage.

This guy, usually a bigshot in the fan circles (because in the convention circuit, an X-Men artist is a rock star), he'll "date" (or, let's face it, hump and dump) several girls in the same community. He wears more faces than Mystique and he has more talents than Mimic, but underneath, he's always the same. He's a villain in hero's clothing. He often wears the worried face of a sensitive forward thinker, but underneath that pretty mask is the twisted visage of a closet misogynist. He's a douche in feminist clothing. He may not even realize what a manipulative monster he is. He's not really that self aware – he's often too self-absorbed to be that purposeful. He wields a sword of deadly charm and a shield of shiny bullshit, and sometimes, it's too much and it fells a single woman, especially because he usually attacks when they're unarmed and vulnerable, and then leaves them bruised on the battlefield.

The battlefield...of love.

(Okay, that was lame.)

This is the type of guy who is as scared of his emotions as groundhogs are of their shadow. They pop their heads out, aren't smart enough to realize that the thing they experienced is just a part of them, and go, "HOLY SHIT! MONSTER! HIDE!" This guy, he doesn't know how to be a real man. He's a professional big kid nerd royalty. The fragile membrane of his ego has been inflated to the point of instability, and he needs constant applications of sexual validation from pretty nerd girls to keep that fragile ego from exploding and blowing his self-esteem to bits. In short, he is totally fucking insufferable.

But what he doesn't understand, what the downfall of this particular breed of low-level monster is, is that we girls, we aren't lone warriors against the world. We have a secret army – each other. And we have a superweapon, if we stop seeing each other as competition and start seeing each other as allies – we have The Grapevine. We just need to activate our secret weapon. It's a simple enough process – we don't need to have superpowers, or fancy rings, or even comically oversized greataxes. It's the easiest thing – all we need to do is to start talking to each other.

The Grapevine works like this: Ororo meets Jean, she hears a name she recognizes – Scott. She thinks back. "Didn't Madelyne say that she dated that Scott dude and he ghosted after they fucked? Shit, this girl should probably know that's a possibility." Ororo tells Jean about Scott's predilection towards douchery, and Jean makes up her mind whether to back out of teaming up with Scott – or proceed with caution, under the knowledge that she can't fully trust who she's joining forces with. And maybe Jean reaches out to Madelyne, and Madelyne and Jean realize they're very similar people – clearly, Scott has a type. And then maybe Jean doesn't date Scott, but she gets a much better relationship out of the deal – a lasting friendship with Madelyne, which, let's face it, is going to be a much more fulfilling relationship than with some whiny mutant with a pretty face. And Scott, well, Jean never calls him again and he's left hanging – and thank god for that, because in the alternate timeline where Jean dates Scott, he just ends up cheating on her with Emma and then giving her psychic crabs (It's a thing. I mean, probably).

Now, the problem with the Grapevine is, it's a viral weapon – one passed down from heroine to heroine. So if, say, Emma doesn't know Jean, Ororo, or Madelyne, she may end up teaming up with Scott.

Thinly veiled analogues involving copyrighted characters that may possibly get me threatened with legal action aside, the Grapevine has been one of the most powerful defensive forces in my day-to-day arsenal. If it weren't for the Grapevine, I wouldn't have had an army of like-minded friends watching my back. If it weren't for the Grapevine, I may have ended up with my heart broken more often (or possibly a bad case of psychic crabs). If it weren't for the Grapevine, I wouldn't even be published in this anthology, and you wouldn't be reading this story right now.

Boys say that us girls gossip too much – maybe we do.
Or maybe we gossip just enough.
And maybe that's our secret weapon.
So pass it on.

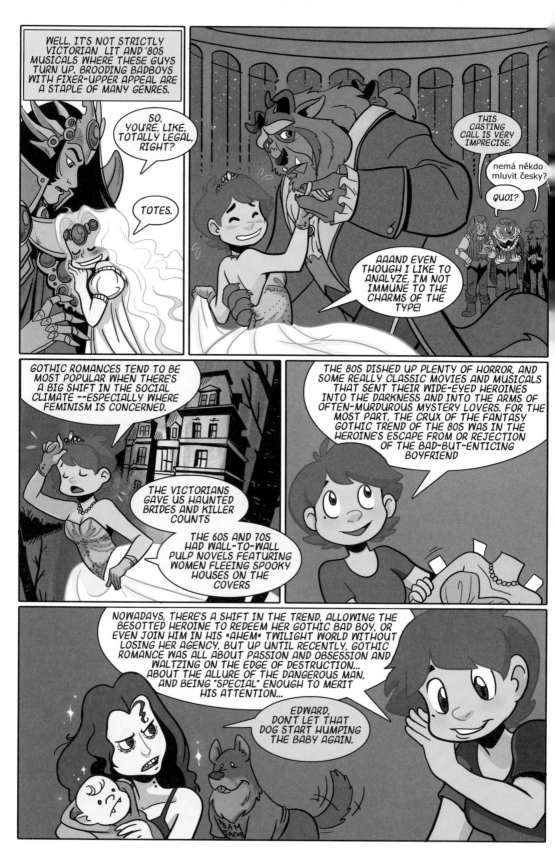

WELL, IT'S NOT STRICTLY VICTORIAN LIT AND '80S MUSICALS WHERE THESE GUYS TURN UP. BROODING BADBOYS WITH FIXER-UPPER APPEAL ARE A STAPLE OF MANY GENRES.

SO, YOU'RE, LIKE, TOTALLY LEGAL, RIGHT?

TOTES.

THIS CASTING CALL IS VERY IMPRECISE.

nemá někdo mluvit česky?

QUOI?

AAAND EVEN THOUGH I LIKE TO ANALYZE, I'M NOT IMMUNE TO THE CHARMS OF THE TYPE!

GOTHIC ROMANCES TEND TO BE MOST POPULAR WHEN THERE'S A BIG SHIFT IN THE SOCIAL CLIMATE --ESPECIALLY WHERE FEMINISM IS CONCERNED.

THE VICTORIANS GAVE US HAUNTED BRIDES AND KILLER COUNTS

THE 60S AND 70S HAD WALL-TO-WALL PULP NOVELS FEATURING WOMEN FLEEING SPOOKY HOUSES ON THE COVERS

THE 80S DISHED UP PLENTY OF HORROR, AND SOME REALLY CLASSIC MOVIES AND MUSICALS THAT SENT THEIR WIDE-EYED HEROINES INTO THE DARKNESS AND INTO THE ARMS OF OFTEN-MURDUROUS MYSTERY LOVERS. FOR THE MOST PART, THE CRUX OF THE FANTASY GOTHIC TREND OF THE 80S WAS IN THE HEROINE'S ESCAPE FROM OR REJECTION OF THE BAD-BUT-ENTICING BOYFRIEND

NOWADAYS, THERE'S A SHIFT IN THE TREND, ALLOWING THE BESOTTED HEROINE TO REDEEM HER GOTHIC BAD BOY, OR EVEN JOIN HIM IN HIS *AHEM* TWILIGHT WORLD WITHOUT LOSING HER AGENCY, BUT UP UNTIL RECENTLY, GOTHIC ROMANCE WAS ALL ABOUT PASSION AND OBSESSION AND WALTZING ON THE EDGE OF DESTRUCTION... ABOUT THE ALLURE OF THE DANGEROUS MAN, AND BEING "SPECIAL" ENOUGH TO MERIT HIS ATTENTION...

EDWARD, DON'T LET THAT DOG START HUMPING THE BABY AGAIN.

TEAM JACOB

THAT WEAKNESS FOR ANGSTY AND CONTROLLING GUYS IS PRETTY UNIVERSAL IN THE GOTHIC GENRE. SO IS STALKING-AS-ROMANTIC-GESTURE, AND THE ONLY-I-CAN-FIX-HIM MENTALITY. NOW, YOU'RE PROBABLY THINKING TO YOURSELF...

"OK, BUT IS IT SEXUAL?"

YEAHHHHH

ALL RIGHT, YES, THANKS FOR THAT. YOU CAN GO NOW. BYE, BYE, BYE.

SHOO

SO IS THE APPEAL OF GOTHIC ROMANCE SEXUAL? WELL, YES AND NO. IT'S ALL ABOUT BROACHING THE TOPIC OF SEX WITHOUT OUTRIGHT ADMITTING IT. THE GOTHIC BADBOY REPRESENTS MYSTERY AND ALLURE: HE'S THE PROMISE OF THINGS NOT YET EXPERIENCED.

HE'S A TESTING GROUND FOR SENSUALITY.

BECAUSE OF THAT, IN ORDER FOR OUR BROODING BEAU TO MAINTAIN HIS ALLURE AND MENACE, THE RELATIONSHIP WITH OUR WIDE-EYED HEROINE CAN NEVER BE EXPLICITLY CONSUMMATED.

IT'S FINE TO HAVE CHRISTINE WAKE UP IN THE PHANTOMS BED, BUT NOT TO SAY OUTRIGHT WHAT, IF ANYTHING, HAPPENED THERE.

CHK-CHAK

AS FOR THE GOTHIC HEROINE, SHE EXISTS IN A TRANSITORY STATE. SHE'S ENTICED BY ROMANCE BUT SHE'S STILL "PURE". SHE'S NAIVE, AND EVEN IF SHE'S CURIOUS, EVEN IF SHE'S TEMPTED TO TRANSGRESS, SHE'S STILL UNTOUCHED.

SHE EXISTS IN PERPETUAL ADOLESCENCE, TEETERING ON THE PRECIPICE OF EXPERIENCE, BUT NEVER FALLING...

...UNTIL SHE DOES.

FOR WHATEVER REASON, IT'S VAMPIRES WHO DOMINATE IN THIS ARENA. MODERN MISSES LIKE BELLA AND BUFFY BOTH BED THEIR BEFANGED BOYFRIENDS

BUCKLE UP, CREAMPUFF

...OR GIRLFRIENDS.

DRACULA IS THE GRAND-DADDY OF 'EM ALL.

THE WHOLE DESPOILED VIRGIN BUSINESS GETS TURNED ON ITS HEAD HERE.

SHARP BITS

FOOTIES

VAMPIRE

SNAP

DRACULA MENACES TWO WOMEN IN PARTICULAR:

LOL, I WONDER IF I COULD MARRY THREE GUYS ALL AT ONCE!

IT'S A UNIX SYSTEM! I KNOW THIS!

LUCY WESTINRA

-CLASSIC WAIF DRESSED IN WHITE,

-LITERALLY EVERYONE IN LOVE WITH HER.

-WASTES AWAY WHILE HER BEVY OF BEAUS WATCH IN HELPLESS HORROR

-BURIED IN HER WEDDING DRESS, COOL METAPHOR, BRO.

-RESURRECTED AS A CHILD-EATING GHOUL AND KILLED BY HER SQUAD OF BOYFRIENDS.

MINA MURRAY

-FEMINIST FORERUNNER WHO CRACKS JOKES ABOUT HOW MUCH SHE CAN EAT

-HAS A JOB AND KEEPS UP WITH MODERN TECH

-LITERALLY EVERYONES SHOULDER TO CRY ON

-ENGAGED TO JONATHAN, WHO IS AWOL IN VAMPIRE COUNTRY

- BOOKS BEFORE BOYS, LADIES. BUT SERIOUSLY, SHE'S LIKE A COOL VICTORIAN HACKER..

BUT WHILE LUCY WASTES AWAY, MINA PACKS HER BAG AND HEADS TO ROMANIA WHERE SHE QUICKLY WEDS AND BEDS HER BORING BEDRIDDEN FIANCEE

GET READY.

BAM

SHE'S MARKED BY DRACULA, BUT SHE'S TAKEN SEX AND SEXUALITY INTO HER OWN HANDS: SHE'S ACTIVE WHERE LUCY WAS PASSIVE

IN THE END, MINA LURES AND DEFEATS THE VAMPIRE, SAVED NOT BY PURITY OR INNOCENCE, BUT BY MATURITY AND EXPERIENCE.

ULTIMATELY, THE APPEAL OF THE BAD BOY LIES IN HIS OTHERNESS. HE'S DIFFERENT FROM THE OTHER MEN IN THE HEROINE'S MUNDANE LIFE AND LIKE HER, HE'S EXCLUDED FROM PATRIARCHAL SOCIETY, AND EVEN THOUGH HE CAN OVERCOMPENSATE IN HIS MASCULINITY, HIS ISOLATION EVOKES OUR SYMPATHY

"IF ONLY PEOPLE HAD BEEN KIND TO HIM!"

"IT'S NOT CREEPY, IT'S ROMANTIC!"

"DOES HE LOVE ME, OR IS HE TRYING TO KILL ME?!"

IT'S ABOUT OBSESSION, AND POSSESION, AND THE FLATTERING SENSE OF SPECIAL-NESS THAT COMES WITH FEELING FIXATION-WORTHY

THE HEROINE IS ISOLATED BY HER SUITOR'S INTEREST, IF SHE WERE TO CHOOSE HIM, IT WOULD MEAN GIVING HERSELF OVER ENTIRELY...

It's meeeee your cathyyy I've come hooome

SOMETIMES EVEN REJECTING HIM ISN'T ENOUGH TO END THE BLACK-HEARTED LOVER'S INFLUENCE. OUR DAMSEL'S DESIRE FOR THE DARKNESS IS WHAT DESTROYS HER.

WHILE SOME MODERN MONSTERS WIND UP DOMESTICATED BY THEIR LADY-LOVES, THE TRADITIONAL STRUCTURE DEMANDS THAT A DARK ROMANCE BE A TRAGEDY.

THE FANTASTIC IS ALLURING, BUT IT CAN'T EXIST ALONGSIDE THE ORIDINARY. IT CAN'T LOVE IN MODERATION OR WITH SELFLESSNESS.

THE MONSTER MUST DIE, OR AT LEAST RETREAT BACK INTO THE SHADOWS, THE DEMON LOVER CAN'T HOLD UP TO THE LIGHT OF DAY.

OUR MODERN LOVE AFFAIR WITH THE GOTHIC IS ALL ABOUT EXPLORING TEMPTATION, BUT ULTIMATELY KEEPING OUR SENSE OF SELF. SARAH KNEW THAT NOTHING COULD BE MORE DELICIOUS THAN STANDING OVER THE GROVELLING GOBLIN KING, AND REALIZING HE HAS NO POWER OVER YOU.

...SO YOU CAN JUST KEEP THAT MAGIC DANCE IN THOSE MAGIC PANTS, BUDDY.

BUK BUK

Never Kiss a Writer

Alicia Contestabile

There's a fine line between art and life. They bleed into each other. Personally, I don't think I can separate the two. I want to make a game that will touch a player, and reveal a relationship's narrative in a way that feels real and true. When I sit down to write, I want to spill my guts like a pixelated blood splatter or the red wine necessary to even begin writing these words.

I wrote these words secretly, sitting across from him, silently, working on a game with the tagline, "this is the untrue story of a love that never was."

I started making games with an open source program called Twine. It's a tool for creating interactive narratives. It can be used to create choose-your-own-adventure type games, or anything that you can create with the use of HTML and CSS that will run in a browser.

When I began working on personal games, I focused on creating experiences that would simulate struggles with mental health to educate and reduce stigma about mental illness. There's a growing movement in games of writers and designers creating small-scale narrative non-fiction games.

In my engagement with the works of independent developers, the most prominently featured works in my research, talks, and workshops are deeply personal games, many of which are Twines, created by folks sharing experiences from their lives. Many of these experiences are very far from casual water-cooler topics or convention networking conversations. Independent developers are tackling extremely tough subjects like racism, sexism, homophobia, transphobia, dysphoria, abuse, mental illness, and other very important, personal issues in autobiographical games.

I'd like to work on some grand opus that didn't involve my life, or myself, or didn't so seamlessly integrate the personal into the professional, but I haven't written that yet. I could write a piece of prose, or I could make a game; I could create a work of interactive fiction, or a text-based game based in reality, exploring relationships.

Sometimes I want to turn off the part of my brain that thinks in words (and, ugh, gross, feelings) and even the part that relates appropriately to other human beings. I want to be engrossed in the process of writing code so much that it's 5 am, and I don't know where the time went, or when the last time I ate was, so it doesn't matter whether or not so-and-so read my text and didn't answer.

More realistically, I'd be sitting watching tutorial videos, tugging on my hair, and chugging coffee, and trying to figure out how to make that exploratory maze game I want to create so I can express what I feel the need to express without saying so god damned much.

I write so many words and they're all characters on a screen, so when I can't see his eyes, I don't know what he's thinking or what the few words he writes mean. Maybe if I could speak his language, I'd understand.

I'm running out of words, and I'm especially running out of code metaphors. No one wants to read another heavy-handed poem about an apocalyptic scenario that's a thinly veiled allegory for your disastrous year-long breakup with your partner.

As a writer of personal narratives, I must admit, it's not necessarily that past experiences are driving the narrative, but maybe the need for a narrative is driving the experiences.

I know I probably drank too much wine that night because I knew the words would flow more freely that way, but was it for the content of that personal game, these words on the page, or the drunken verbal dance I eventually did in his bedroom around the topic of 'us'?

Say I wanted to write about my travels, and what I learned about love and sex through going overseas. If someone asked me, I might jokingly reply, "foreskin." Am I allowed to make a game about foreskin?

In personal games, is it the humor or the heartbreak that truly touches? The obvious answer is both. I might write about the silliness of his panty fetish or the seriousness of the deceit that concealed it in the first place.

I also might write about the vulnerability of pegging your partner and the horrifyingly hilarious aftermath of play fighting over who is going to clean the mess.

I know these are the things I'm not supposed to write. Sex is supposed to be serious. In games, it can be an option that follows the correct choices on a dialogue tree, or stilted mechanical movements of pixels on a screen. But it's not simply the simulation that I want to portray in a game; it's the way a relationship felt. It's the voice, the laughter, the nervousness, and the play.

Imagine a two-player game about virginity and inexperience where you're trying to mash randomly generated genitals together on the screen but the controls are entirely broken until you initiate dialogue or laughter with your partner.

It's not that sexual representations of relationships are the most interesting or necessary material for personal games about relationships. In a way, sex can be less personal than other activities. It's possible to have the most intimate of relationships with someone that you've never had the chance to experience sexually.

Is there a way to make a mechanic that reflects the emotional affect of the intimate act of wild sex versus painting each other's nails while talking about love? Are you more intimate with the person that you're sexually engaged with or the person that you connect with and engage with most? Is true intimacy about sharing your secrets? What does that make of me for sharing them in a game, or in this very book?

I'm still trying to navigate the space between keeping secrets and making personal games. This entire writing process has been one long metaphorical experiment in meta-narrative. I know I'm not supposed to tell other people's secrets. But I'm already breaking all the rules of games by definition.

What if you dropped two players into a simulated conversation of a contrived relationship where they were given choices of what to say next to a stranger on the Internet? Imagine a game where your character wants to tell their partner that they love them, or what about being dropped into the middle of a break up? Maybe the weird conversations we have with each other online could be a game in itself.

Relationships themselves are not games, but there are always rules to an extent. Sex isn't necessarily a game, though it could be, and it's ultimately playful.

There are also the conversations that don't fit the narrative. They're the ones you have with your eyes. Those conversations don't necessarily fit into a purely text-based game.

How can I textually represent the look in someone's eyes? The game we play where we look into each other's eyes and try to make the other one cry when we're saying goodbye, and the laughter that breaks out between us when one of us wins.

There are a lot of questions that emerge when working on personal games, or any kind of personal writing I suppose. It's hard to know where to start, where to end, or especially, what to reveal. How do you share your own personal truth without revealing the secrets of others? Do secrets function like the public domain? They're copyrighted for a set amount of time, and then when everyone's had a chance to heal and to deal, they become free game.

It's as if there's some kind of arbitrary rule of thumb that you're supposed to wait at least a year after the demise of a relationship to write about it. Does that mean I'm not allowed to write about a current relationship?

I remember he was upset by the thought of me writing about our relationship and specifically our conversations, in the conversation that began this very dialogue.

What if writing is a way to move on? Is that just what journals are for? Is the key to this conundrum to be selectively succinct and only reveal snippets of secrets?

If I said that his hands were soft, and his kisses were rough, but don't say what he did with those hands, or what came out of his mouth, or that he bit me and I liked it. Is that fair?

What is fair game? I want to know how long I'm supposed to let a story age before I pour it. Is there some sort of calculation, like half the amount of time you dated? How does that account for the whirlwind weekend romance? Does it depend on whether or not you're still in that person's life? Is it whether the person will be identifiable by anyone? Being so far removed from an old love's social circle might have worked prior to social networking. But things get especially tricky when you're in the same industry.

Furthermore, is it cheap to rely on romantic love (or sex) for inspiration? There are so many questions but no answer here. Most importantly, do I have to go on a bunch of really horrible Tinder dates if I want to write about sex, love, and relationships?

All because I can't tell you about what it was like when he bit my lip during our first kiss, or when I took his virginity, or when we went on that date with a couple from Craigslist, or when we were poly and I took a secondary partner without permission. Are these my secrets to tell? What is an appropriate amount of distance between a writer and their subject before they can reveal that they were the master and the other was pet?

But, honestly, enough with all of these questions. You should know better than to kiss a writer. They always tell.

WOOZY WINKS AND PLASTIC MAN

Why I Know My Partner is Really a Superhero

Trina Robbins, illustration by Jessica Paoli

Superheroes and superheroines never get married (Reed and Sue Richards are exceptions, but that's because they are both superheroes). because then their spouses would find out their secret identities. It's hard to hide such things from your hubby or wifey if you are out until all hours of the night fighting villains. However, I suspect – nay, I know! – that my beloved partner of many years has a secret identity that he has tried to hide from me.

He is secretly Plastic Man.

No, really. And here is proof:

He is often up all night fighting crime.

Well, he pretends that he has deadlines that keep him up until 5 am, but I know that he actually fights crime until 4, and then rushes back to the drawing table, looking sufficiently haggard so that I will believe he's meeting deadlines.

But why Plastic Man?

Plastic Man is very tall, and he can stretch like a rubber band to become even taller. My partner, Steve, is very tall, and sometimes, when I ask him to reach for things on the highest shelf that I can't reach without putting life and limb in danger by standing on a phone book on top of a chair, he can reach them without standing on *anything*. So he must be stretching like a rubber band.

But then, why Plastic Man and not Reed Richards?

Reed Richards is a wimp, and he's already married. Reed Richards has no sense of humor. Plastic Man has a sense of humor, and my partner has a great sense of humor. Ergo, he is Plastic Man. Here are some more reasons:

Plastic Man wears sunglasses all the time. Sunglasses on a man are very sexy and make him look like a jazz musician. Steve is not a jazz musician, but he is a bass player and loves jazz. Once when we were traveling in Paris, Steve lost his glasses in some medieval cathedral, and so was forced to wear sunglasses all the time, even at night. He looked very sexy, but he kept bumping into things.

Plastic Man is colored red and yellow, so that when he becomes, say, a chair or a rug, the chair and the rug are colored red and yellow.

Steve has a red and yellow aloha shirt that I found for him at a thrift shop, because I'm the thrift shop queen of San Francisco.

Plastic Man has a sidekick named Woozy Winks. Woozy Winks is very short and funny looking. I am very short and hopefully, not *that* funny looking. Also, I hope I am more than a sidekick.

Superman traditionally goes into phone booths to change from his suit and tie into his blue tights with the red S on the chest. Plastic Man never goes into telephone booths because he doesn't wear a suit and tie and is always Plastic Man in red and yellow; thus, no changing of clothes.

Steve also never goes into phone booths. Of course, there are no phone booths to go into anymore, but that's beside the point.

And finally: you never see Plastic Man and Steve together at the same time!

No Country
for Old Mentors

Soraya Roberts, illustration by Melissa Kay

The original mentor wasn't much of one. A friend and advisor to
Odysseus, Mentor was left in charge of the king's son when he went
to war. Pretty much the second he appeared he was asked, "what
mischief are you raking up?" A few hundred pages later he was deemed
a "blowhard." It wasn't until Athena transformed into him that Mentor
did much of anything. She was the source of encouragement, not him.

Thirteen centuries later true mentors are still hard to come by.
Mentoring means having the time and the inclination to guide
someone you don't have to. I only ever seemed to recognize mine in
retrospect – the teacher who first encouraged me to write, the editor
who shaped that writing. In one of my old jobs I was asked to choose
my ideal mentor. "Joan Didion," I said. But she never showed up.

In 2014, Forbes reported that women have a hard time finding
mentors and, when they do, they benefit less from them than men.
Other studies have shown that women are judged more harshly than
men, which may explain why they are not favored as protégées. Or
maybe it has to do with sex. Not their sex, sex. A 1999 paper in the
Journal of Applied Psychology discovered that female protégées were
less likely to engage in social activities with male mentors than female
mentors, suggesting it was "for fear that the interaction would be
misconstrued as sexual in nature." Or maybe I just shouldn't have met

my "mentor" in his hotel room at midnight.

I first met Aldrich Sumner when I interviewed him for a story a year before I moved to New York. Not many people around me knew who he was, but I had been following his films for a decade. The day of our interview I was wearing an old tweed jacket which still had a pink button pinned to it from my freshman year in university, around the time I first heard of him. "Stop staring at my boobs," it read. "I promise not to," Aldrich replied.

We had a cordial chat. His publicist kept interrupting us with an irritating live countdown and before I had completed my questions, my time was up. At that point Aldrich slipped me a piece of paper. "Here's my email address," he said. "Feel free to send me the rest." There was nothing prurient about it. He was around 20 years older than me and worked with beautiful women all the time. I assumed he simply took a paternalistic shine to me. And I had just written a script. Kismet.

So I wrote him. And he wrote me back. And I wrote him again and he wrote me back again, ad infinitum. We emailed about books and movies and life. I told him about my script and he agreed to read it. This was the one time I appeared to be acknowledging I had a mentor while actually having one. I clung to it. Even after he first mentioned sex, I clung. The pathos did not escape me. It was pathetic to believe my association with this man was the only thing imbuing me with any artistic credibility. Dropping him meant dropping any chance I had at being a real screenwriter. And I was inconsequential enough in New York not to want to lose that as well.

Aldrich didn't live in the city but he was often in New York for work. In the middle of the summer he flew into town for a week of rehearsals. One particularly sultry evening, I was reading alone in bed and suddenly craved a chocolate milkshake from Burgers N' Shakes – but only if I could drink it while sitting on a stoop on 9th Avenue watching all the late night foodies stroll by. I figured Aldrich would be into that sort of thing, so I texted him. It was 11 pm. He didn't write back until an hour later.

-Did you already go out?

-yep!! it was delish. but i was wilting so i came back and am now ensconced in my book. sucks you weren't around earlier, i was craving company.

-And now? Come to my place and read with me.

A booty call. Clearly. Unless he read with other people a lot? At midnight?

-ill come chat if yer in hells kitchen...

-I'm at the Grand – get in a cab and I'll pay your cab both ways.

Fuck off "pay for my cab"...

-ugh, yer killing me. fine, but ill pay for my own cab thanks ;) what room?

-1424. bring your book.

I knew I shouldn't go. And I knew that if I did go I wouldn't need a book. But I wanted to see his room. I knew it was inane, but all I had ever experienced in New York were parquet floors and crack heads shooting up in the doorway outside my window. I wanted a piece of Aldrich's life. I wanted to touch his bamboo flooring.

I changed out of my dress into a T-shirt and jeans – it was midnight, I didn't want to push it. I waved down a cab and felt giddy as it sped down the highway passed the Hudson River. I sunk low in my seat and leaned my head back to watch the street lights glow by. The driver glanced at me in his rear view and I fleetingly thought that he might have sized me up as a call girl. But call girls always wore red lipstick and little black dresses, right?

At the Grand I took the elevator to the 6th floor. There was no one in it at that hour. As I approached Aldrich's room at the end of the fluorescent-lit hallway, I felt as though I should be wearing a trench coat and heels. As it turned out, even jeans set the bar too high.

Aldrich was in his pajamas. "She exists," he said, before I walked into an awkward half hug. He motioned me into his room, which appeared to be almost solely occupied by a king-sized bed. I'm certain the symbolism escaped neither of us. I sat down in the chair furthest away from the bed while Aldrich sat against it. Literally, figuratively, he was supported by it. I didn't know what to say so I asked if he had a minibar. He pointed to something even better: a mini-confectionary. It was full of chocolate bars, but I grabbed the jar of jelly beans.

"Can I take one of these?" I asked

"Help yourself," he said.

I don't even like jelly beans. They were pretty, though, and I didn't want to deliberate over what to eat while he sat staring at my butt. So we shared. Passing the jar back and forth, we talked about his film and the actors in it, many of whom I knew. I brought up my script. He hadn't read it yet, but he complimented my manicure.

"I thought you were staying in Hell's Kitchen, by the way," I said. "At least, I think you told me that."

"I probably said that to get you to come over to my place."

He kept slipping in sexual innuendos. I kept changing the subject.

"I know, you have your commitment," he said.

"Yes, so that is never going to happen."

"30 and you've settled."

"I don't consider it settling. You were married. You didn't consider it settling."

"I was pressured into it, kind of. You wouldn't have to worry about money if you were with me."

"Did you really just say that?"

At that point I got up to use the bathroom. It was clean and minimalist and modern like the rest of the room and it looked like no one had used it. I didn't even see a toothbrush. When I returned, I stopped at the picture window near the foot of the bed and spied on the people in the luxury apartment opposite. It was an elegant affluent couple, two people who looked like they had never needed a mentor in their lives. Aldrich got up and stood next to me. When he moved too close, I leaned away.

"You're funny," he said. I was surprised he wasn't more interesting. He was famous for his interesting dialogue.

I left soon after that.

"I want a real hug this time," Aldrich said at the door. "Not a 20-minute one, just not a half-assed one."

I gave him a half-assed one. I was disappointed that our night didn't turn out like Bob and Charlotte's in *Lost in Translation*. I wrote as much to my best friend. *The relationship between the two of them worked because he didn't make it about sex,* she wrote back, *and in real life I feel like if you have an older man and a younger woman hanging out together in a hotel, it will be very rare that the older guy won't make it about sex.*

I stopped writing to Aldrich after that. A couple of years later I met a female producer who offered to look at my script. She read it within the week and gave me advice almost immediately after. We sent countless emails back and forth. We even spoke on the phone. I am preparing to send her script ideas as I write this. And in the year we have been talking, not once has she mentioned sex.

I DON'T KNOW WHAT I WANT OUT OF A RELATIONSHIP.

Pop Culture Metaphor

WORDS: FIONNA ADAMS PICTURES: JEN VAUGHN

MY EMOTIONAL VOCABULARY IS LACKING, SO I LEAN ON POP CULTURE, ESPECIALLY COMICS, AS METAPHORS.

Fionna Adams @letao_nox · Jul 21
Bojack Horseman's parents are my parents.
↻ 10 ★ 28

Tina Tomorrow @tuhmarrow
Oh. My. GOD!

Hubble Snubs @not_a-spook
Yikes. You are strong.

IT'S EASY TO POINT TO A SCENE IN SOMETHING AND SAY "THAT" AND PEOPLE GET IT.

I STARTED READING COMICS IN COLLEGE, BOTH SUPERHERO AND CREATOR-OWNED. CREATOR-OWNED STORIES HIT CLOSER TO HOME, THOUGH, SO I TEND TO READ THOSE MORE.

CASANOVA IS THE KIND OF COMIC THAT HAS MULTIPLE LAYERS OF UNDERSTANDING.

CASANOVA

I DUG THAT LAYER DEALING WITH FAMILY'S EXPECTATIONS FOR YOU.

KINDA LIKE THIS

MOM, I'M TRANS. MY NAME IS FIONNA NOW.

NO, IT'S NOT

AND WHAT ABOUT MY GRANDKIDS?

WHAT GRAND-KIDS?!

IF CASANOVA QUINN CAN HANDLE THAT WHILE BEING A MASTER-CLASS THIEF IN SPACE, I CAN HANDLE IT HERE...

RIGHT?

A Geek Girl Room of Your Own

Ramblings of Geek Girl and Playwright Crystal Skillman

HELP ME, EVIL BLENDER, YOU'RE MY ONLY HOPE

You never know what's going to happen.

I, however, after a few bad boyfriends, and one real heart-breaker (who of course used his heart-breaking abilities to finally break up with me), was certain of one thing:

"You're going to be alone the rest of your life, you're never going to get married. You're going to create and thrive on your talent" (yes, I talked like this back then).

This was a pep speech in front of the mirror, of course.

After all I was a GEEK growing up in the 90s. Being an outsider and weirdo was my thing!

Flash forward to the dorm room of Parsons School of Design. That's where I landed studying photography and theater at Eugene Lang. There I became best friends with a pink haired girl named Gretchen Van Lente. We were both geek girls and we were RIDICULOUS.

We ate a lot of junk food between projects, naturally, made videos of fake talk shows, drew comics in which we were married to They Might Be Giants, always went to see They Might be Giants, and I even went to her house in Ohio for spring break. She always kept saying that I should meet her brother Fred. He LOVED They Might Be Giants, and

Woody Allen movies (the early crazy ones like I did – and let's keep in mind Woody's true nature had yet to shine).

And my reaction was this: LOVE IS A HORRIBLE, INSANE LIE. The mirror speech still stood as far as I was concerned.

"WHEN SOMEONE ASKS YOU IF YOU'RE A GOD, YOU SAY YES"

Somehow at some point, I got a call out of nowhere from Fred. WHAT?! A company was turning *Tranquility*, a wonderful comic Fred had written about a girl with a talking gun kicking ass on a moon base, into an animated CD-ROM (Again, it's the 90s, people). He was calling me to be the voice of the Evil Blender in an episode. I explained to him that I wasn't an actor. I was studying theater and wrote plays, but didn't I act in them. He just kept saying he thought I'd be great and our conversations were going on a long time and oh my god... what was happening?

We were on the phone for AN HOUR?!!

So at the end of our call I took advice from the greatest Geek rom-com of all times: *GHOSTBUSTERS*. "When someone asks you if you're a God, you say yes." So I said "Yes, let's meet about this comic, I'll be your Evil Blender."

Fred was on his way.

I was getting dressed.

Is this a date?

Is it a date when someone asks you to be the voice of their Evil Blender in space?

Fred showed up without the script.

It's a date.

The "date" itself was quite epic. By the end of it – that first kiss sealed it but... WHERE THE HELL DO THINGS GO FROM HERE?!

DAMAGED GEEK GIRL HEART VS. GEEK GIRL CONFIDENCE – FIGHT!

You see, as excited as I was, I knew I had to be willing to balance my damaged Geek Girl heart. The Girl in the Mirror had a lot to say.

She would rather that I cut things off or "be expected to fail" because that's what happened before. At least that is predictable! At least then I wouldn't TRY and FEEL like a REAL MESS.

But what is failure? In seventh grade I professed to liking my best friend Damien. He met me in our classroom after school, smiled, that KIND, KIND "OH YOU" SMILE but it was clear this was a no-go. I was so embarrassed, I opened the doors to the coat closet in the room and just went in there and closed the door behind me. He patiently waited until I came out, then sat with me and said it was okay.

What he meant, what I couldn't understand then, is that things work and don't work, for mysterious reasons, and it's a balance or that's what I've found… between listening and loving who you are but also being willing to change behaviors that haven't worked before. It's total balls to the walls, cue the Disney-Song-Part-of-Your-World shit and total humility. Willing to admit you're wrong, but change to make YOU the better you that YOU want to invest in.

Calm. Breathe. Know you have TIME. You do! There is time to have these relationships. And I do believe each one MAKES YOU WHO YOU ARE. They are pretty important. Even the crazy ones.

For instance, I had the boyfriend who would send me BOXES OF FORTUNE COOKIES and FLOWERS out of nowhere and SEVEN PAGES OF HANDWRITTEN letters and it was like WHAT?!! Jackpot, here's the prince, let's go, fight, win, DONE!

Uh… no. When he broke up with me it was like lightning. It was OUT OF NOWHERE. Also, my dad at the time was in the hospital. Oh yeah, and it was New Year's Eve in Disneyland and the confetti was falling. Oh, and I was staying at this crazy-breaking-up-with-me-jerk parent's house. And we drove there and had to drive back (from Florida!!) with his sister and her red neck boyfriend and they were just mad I didn't drive shift. CLASSY, people, CLASSY.

What a sucky experience but in dating this guy I discovered the All-I'm-Gonna-Do-Is-Romance-You-To-Death Guy might be a little bonkers in the head.

SOMEONE WHO LOVES YOU

While I'm pretty insanely confident with many things, I'm also a bit of a mess. Ok, I'm a huge mess. But you know what I'm talking about with the RAPID GEEK GIRL INSECURITY right? I just worried. ALL THE TIME!! Was I doing everything right?!!! Am I? Well... as long as you make choices in life you are! So I've found it's better to go for it, and do something even perhaps wrong. What I discovered when I met Fred, as our relationship began to grow, was that someone who LOVES YOU will TELL YOU when there's something that upsets them. Not everyone's idea of relationships is to break up with you on the start of the New Year at a theme park. For the right person in your life, it's actually not a big deal for them to express themselves! And that's pretty normal! For me, I needed that. Slowly I began to let those *Tiny Furniture* years slip away... I was gaining GEEK GIRL CONFIDENCE.

HOUSE OF COMICS & PLAYS

When Fred and I first dated, he lived in Brooklyn on Webster Place. There he roomed with comic book creators Steve Ellis (who co-created/ drew *Tranquility!*), Stew Novak, and Ryan Dunlavey (who draws and co-created *Action Philosophers*, as well as *Action Presidents* with Fred), AND comic book creator Jamal Igle was a frequent visiter!

It was creative and insane... a kind of artistic *Animal House*. It was fun and unpredictable, and everyone had a larger than life personality. So You-Know-Who, still armed with her best friend and art school confidante Gretchen, felt at home. Finally I didn't feel like such a freak! I was constantly surrounded and inspired by the act of making comics.

It was there... and I hope the guys don't mind me saying this, I guess because I was becoming their friend, I was seeing another side to this whole thing as they were really open with me about their lives and relationships.

I was beginning to see that guys – especially those in geek culture – the ones loving it, creating it, and influencing it – have it just as hard. They shared about exes (sometimes bringing down shoeboxes with pictures to show me), and who they were dating now, and I saw the struggles. Everyone has to go through it. And I saw each of them through their own miraculous journeys find someone, even if it took awhile, which was pretty amazing. I think because they stayed true to who they were the whole time.

BOOTH BABE

From the start, I'd go with Fred to comic book conventions, being his "booth babe." It was one of my most favorite things – to see him sign his work, meet his fans. I had never really traveled the world. Now through productions of my plays, or by traveling with Fred to comic-cons, I was going all over the place. That Geek Girl Confidence grew EVEN MORE as my world SUPER EXPANDED SO QUICKLY! I really related to the cosplayers and fans, coming together to share their loves, obsessions, passions. I loved their dedication in meeting creators. So much so that I wrote my play *GEEK!* inspired by these travels and incredible souls.

What I think I related to the most with the cosplayers was how all the girls and women still had their Geek Girl Vulnerability (even old school Slave Leias all have one thing in common, no matter what their body shape, they ALL hold their exposed stomachs as they walk in that weird gold plated outfit). The point is – these ladies were BOLD in how they expressed themselves. In each cosplayer, you saw a bit of their real selves underneath – but the delight in embracing that and saying "Yeah, that's me but I'm also THIS." Truly. It's like Virginia Woolf meets Wonder Woman out there. I'm talking a geek girl room of your own. WE DO BELONG.

So I started as a booth babe. But now, this past year at Denver Comic Con? I just had my own table right along with Fred. There, Trina Robbins, who is just, well, a GENIUS, also took me aside and said she loves how much I love Fred but that I don't always have to mention him on panels. "You're Crystal Skillman," she said, and that's enough. Fred was there listening and he jumped in agreeing!

So… okay… um… confidence and love… how does that finally go together? How do we take this confidence into the big, bad universe?

I think looking for a connection in the real world is tough because the real world is tough. Like shitballs crazy. Reality is just not as much fun as the plays I write or your own passion. We can't rewrite real life. It's always there. Accepting reality is important to grow, BUT choosing how you want to live *within it* is up to you. And allows change to happen! And dreams.

Let yourself dream, be creative, and know that tomorrow

is not today. Your Geek Girl-ness – all of it! The insecurity and confidence – together balances into YOU. Embrace it all. Be open, share yourself with the world. It's okay to be the hero of your own journey. Be a leader – take chances in dating just like you would do in all aspects of your life.

But also, you can realize that this is "all for the moment". I realized as my relationship with Fred grew, just as Fred realized too, we couldn't answer the "forever" question. We felt like we'd be together forever, but we can't make promises like that to each other. What matters more is us as people, and how we care for each other and have fun! Even when we moved in together, into our own apartment, even when we got married, and woke up today and started writing in our little treehouse of a house, nothing really changed. We were, we are, still Fred and Crystal and Crystal and Fred. Living in a house of comic books and plays.

And we both advise you – if someone asks you to voice an evil blender in an animation of their comic book, YOU SAY YES.

BEFORE I STARTED HIGH SCHOOL, I THOUGHT A *LOT* ABOUT TEENAGE ROMANCE.

I WOULD WATCH A LOT OF TV AND MOVIES WITH THAT SORT OF THING, AND THOUGHT THAT WOULD HAPPEN TO *ME*.

WHEN I STARTED GRADE 9 HOWEVER, I WAS HIT WITH THE *HARD, COLD* REALITY

TEENAGERS SUCK.

I DON'T THINK THEY KNOW WHAT LOVE IS *AT ALL.*

YOU SURE KNOW A LOT ABOUT COMICS... *FOR A GIRL.*

YOU'D BE *CUTER* IF YOU WERE SHORTER.

MOST OF MY FRIENDS HAVE BEEN IN RELATIONSHIPS BY NOW. I THOUGHT THERE WAS SOMETHING *WRONG* WITH ME.

BUT THERE ISN'T.

I HAVE **PLENTY** OF FRIENDS AND FAMILY WHO LOVE ME JUST AS WELL.

PLATONIC RELATIONSHIPS ARE FUN AND DON'T COME WITH THE **DRAMA** THAT RELATIONSHIPS DO.

SO IF YOU'RE LIKE ME AND YOU'RE IN HIGH SCHOOL, DON'T **RUSH** TO FIND LOVE, IT'S **NOT WORTH IT.**

JUST FOCUS ON **YOURSELF** AND LOVE WILL FIND **YOU** EVENTUALLY.

END.

May I Admire
You Again Today?

A story of rolling 4DMG and finding love

Twiggy Tallant

Is it a cliche to call oneself a dreamer?

Is it a cop out?

A way to absolve oneself of the responsibility of normalcy, or one's inability to conform to societal expectations?

Is it an animal instinctual defence system?

I used my imagination to escape my reality. I dug through the depths of the pages of the books I read and the cult classic films I memorized to create a colourful world of obscure music, partners in crime, worshipping love interests, and of course, beautiful, spontaneous, magical circumstance.

I lived through the anti-social, punk rock, strong female characters I idolized. I wrote my life away like Veronica Sawyer in *Heathers*, I danced around my room to obscure vinyl like Enid from *Ghost World*, I dressed myself in the spirit of Iona from *Pretty in Pink*. And with those characters came their dashing knights. The unsuspecting nerdy best friend, the psychotic rebel, the unassuming music expert. I wasn't interested in love, I wanted the story. I didn't care for being liked, I wanted to be craved like a drug. I wanted that "God I would have died for you" adoration. Where was my homicidal Christian Slater, my shy

Steve Buscemi? Where was my Duckie?

I spent my whole life angrily pondering *Pretty in Pink* Andy's decision to choose the rich square over the impeccably dressed, wit for days, 80s dreamboat best friend of hers. The popular boy states to her face that "I'm not really into this shit, you know" regarding her interests, listens to his friends and ditches her before prom so she's forced to go alone, and yet he wins. Fucking bollocks! And yet how guilty we all are of making this exact error. I think boys think we've figured it out, like we've cracked the relationship code. WRONG SIRS. We are just as useless and lost. Mapless and without cheats. Vulnerable. Trying and failing, having to go back to the first level and start from the beginning of the game.

Being the friend of the pretty girl, or the cool girl, or the slutty girl, I played the sidekick card well. I was always looked past, which worked in my favour because I wasn't built for my environment. I had no shared interests with the boys in my neighbourhood. And the rare gems I found in the quicksand that is Scarborough, Ontario, I very selfishly tried to keep so close that through my own naivety I ate a few souls.

FULL DISCLOSURE: The first 'Duckie' to enter my life I destroyed with my bare hands like a pug that you love so much that you squeeze it to death. I wrung his neck with a friendship I could not live without. He loved me and was everything I had ever dreamed up. But I was not willing to lose what we had, a synchronicity to this day I haven't been able to replicate, and I had no experience on this side of the fence. I handled it awfully, we both did. I didn't know how to give up my best friend for an experiment that had failed me thus far. I lost him forever.

But I digress. This is my first "feel it in your knees" cult classic moment story.

So, I'll start by saying the first thing I remember about him was the way he spoke. His quick wit that most nerds have obtained as their own brand of defence. He was tall, with very sharp Eastern European facial features. He had big hazel eyes and the 'my nerd activities are exclusively indoors' pale skin. I instantly decided that he was to be my next victim. He was going to speak to me. He was going to entertain me for the duration of my time spent in this Games Workshop. He had no choice, he was on the clock, and I wasn't one to take no for an answer.

I did not want to enter the Games Workshop in the Eaton Centre. The cesspool of tourists, trending brand names and tragic consumerism at its most gluttonous made my body twitch uncontrollably. However the *Warhammer* playing community could not have hoped for a better public dingy cellar dwelling. In the darkest depths of Toronto's downtown mall attraction, the exclusive stubby lower level hall that led to the subway hosted a Games Workshop, a massage parlour and a convenience store. It sounds far worse than it was, but facts are facts.

I had been picked up from my tattoo parlour day job by my high school friend Stephanie and her boyfriend Jordan. They insisted, to my dismay, on entering the dreaded sheeple lair. We were almost out scot-free, less than 10 feet from the door to the subway station to take us all back to Scarborough when Jordan locked eyes with the neatly stacked boxes of toys and bottles of model paint. I resisted. I had been told countless times by my skater friends to avoid this place at all costs. Even though we played videogames for afternoons at a time and read comic books, *Warhammer* was, on some form, a different nerd level. There were degrees of nerd, and this particular activity was 'too much,' whatever that meant, and therefore off limits. Basically there are subcultures within the nerd world, and they didn't interact with each other.

Lorand Vagaszki had a confidence about him that impressed me. He wasn't cowering to my overcompensating extroverted shtick. He was keeping up. He didn't blink, I noticed this because I never did. I fed off the way someone looked at me. But when he smiled I could feel it in the middle of my esophagus.

I was draped in the social rebel attire of the time. My quest was to attempt to redefine the term 'outrageous.' I had submerged myself fully into the baptismal Art School pool. I was a head to toe dark psychedelic social experiment. I had risen from the ashes of years of torment, and became a mysterious, obnoxious, gothic, technicoloured mess. A deviant. I went from having no voice to having the loudest one. I liked this version of myself, I felt safe with her. But about as safe as you would be with a loaded gun in your pocket. I decided to wear my damage on my sleeve. Nothing could have prepared me for the consequences that would come from such a decision. But I wasn't prepared to continue hiding, and I was drunk with my new power. I was going to do whatever I wanted, and at this moment I wanted this man's attention.

I could feel my mall allotted time with my red-shirted prey slipping through my paint covered fingers. I was sat in the 'painting station' area painting a warrior I had been given and I was living for my new art project. Lorand had been working on his rat army and I couldn't help but playfully tease him. I was deflecting from the fact that I found him painting his army of miniature rat warrior models incredibly attractive. The rats reminded me of novels I would read religiously growing up by Brian Jacques, about medieval woodland creatures who often battled injustice throughout the kingdoms of their fictional world.

My feelings had begun to confuse me. Was my own game backfiring? Keep it together, girl! If I had to put my finger on it, I'd say it was his focus. The detail he was putting into his figures was exquisite. I caught myself staring at him while he painted. The way he carefully held the tiny plastic figurine in his fingers, the precision of his brush. His colour schemes slayed me.

Closing time. We all have to leave. Shit. I remember saying our goodbyes and thank yous. I knew that I would be back. This was the time before the virtual stalking abilities of social media, even cell phones weren't fully mandatory. So if you wanted to get to know someone, you had to continuously run into them until you knew them well enough to ask them to hang out, maybe then get a phone number. Stalking before it was cool, and I had turned this creepy activity into an art form.

I was back within the week. I could not stop thinking about him. I had gone to get some lunch in the food court with him when I blurted out that I wanted to take him out. He turned me down. I wasn't even phased. I proceeded to show up, almost every day that I worked. I changed my route to and from work so that I would come in and out of that hole in the ground next to Games Workshop and pretended that it had always been this way. I made friends with all the guys he worked with, and a bunch of the regulars. I would go in and hang out without him even being there. I honestly loved hanging out in Games Workshop. I learned how *Warhammer* was played and it was always so impressive to see how people were customizing and painting their models. Soon enough I was being invited to hang out with his friends, which he had little say about. I infiltrated his life. I was in, even if I was only a wallflower. His friends knew how I felt and teased him about it in front of me all the time. I relished all of it.

A month and half had gone past and I had given up the persistent hunt. One day a few of us went to the bar across from the Eaton Centre after work. Usually he would go off with the guys but this time he was standing on the subway platform with me. We were so rarely alone. He looked at me and said "What are you doing? Do you want to hang out?" I was jumping out of my skin but very coolly responded with "Sure." We proceeded to take the long way to his place listening to Stone Temple Pilots and Bush on his MP3 player. I rested my legs on his lap on the bus. I knew then I had won. I had run him out like a lion chasing a gazelle. We got to his house and ended up lying on the basement couch together, watching *Orgazmo*. We weren't even touching, a medium size dog could have snuggled up between us with ease. I was over waiting. I rolled over and kissed him. We proceeded to make out for the duration of the film and fell asleep on the couch.

So how do our heroines end their love affairs? Enid gets on a legendary bus to nowhere, Veronica lights a cigarette in admiration while she watches her beau blow himself up, and Iona conforms to a social norm to date this nice guy. It was never supposed to be a beautiful ending. It was never going to last forever. Prince Charming doesn't come save you. You can only take what your moments give you and anticipate the ones to come. The inevitable ending doesn't take away the moments that melt our hearts, scar our souls, and change our lives.

You may ask how my "I live to like you" cult classic moment went? We dated for over a year. He had a magic black and white cat called Figaro. He painted designs on my nails in model paint and I worshipped him like a God.

Everything sir. It was everything.

1993

I AM 17.
I AM IN LOVE.
MY LOVE IS
(SCIENCE) FICTION.

TECHNICALLY,
THE PERSON I LOVE
IS A GUY NAMED PAUL,
WHO PLAYS
FRANK-N-FURTER
IN THE TORONTO
BLOOR CINEMA CAST OF
THE ROCKY HORROR
PICTURE SHOW.

BUT, LET'S BE HONEST,
I DON'T GIVE A SHIT
ABOUT PAUL.
I WOULD RUN
IN HORROR IF I
SAW HIM OUT
OF MAKE UP.

I LOVE
FRANK-N-FURTER,
SWEET...
HAUNTER
OF DREAMS.

THAT SUMMER,
I HAVE MY LAST BOYFRIEND, "A".
HE WEARS FANGS MORE THAN
HE PROBABLY SHOULD.
HE BUYS ME A MEMBERSHIP
AT THE LOCAL
GOTH BAR.
THIS IS HOW
I FIND OUT
HE DOESN'T
KNOW MY
LAST NAME.

SANCTUARY
VAMPIRE SEX BAR
K.M. TUMACHÍ
- MEMBER -

WHEN I KISS "A",
I THINK ABOUT PAUL AND
FRANK-N-FURTER.

JUST BECAUSE A PERSON
DOESN'T EXIST,
DOESN'T MEAN THEY
CAN'T TAKE UP
RESIDENCE IN
THE BASEMENT
OF YOUR
AORTA,
CRANK CALL
YOUR BRAIN
EVERY
FIFTEEN
MINUTES.

DO NOT UNDERESTIMATE
THE POWER OF LOVE
THAT IS NOT TECHNICALLY "REAL".

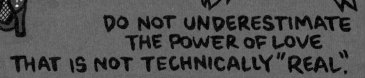

1994 I AM 18, FINALLY.
I AM A STUDENT AT MONTREAL'S McGILL U, STILL IN LOVE WITH FRANK-N-FURTER.
I HAVE JOINED THE RHPS CAST AT THE CINEMA DU PARIS.

I START OFF AS MAGENTA, THE MAD MAID. PRESUMABLY BECAUSE THAT'S WHERE THEY PUT THE CHUBBY GIRLS.

THE CAST IS FULL OF APPROPRIATELY SHADY CHARACTERS, INCLUDING "EDDIE", A LOTHARIO WASTOID, WHO MAKES ME MICROWAVE BROWNIES AND SHOWS ME PICTURES OF "JANET" HIS GIRLFRIEND.

AND "RIFF RAFF" WHO STUFFS LOVE NOTES IN MY POCKETS THAT I'M PRETTY SURE ARE RIPPED OFF FRENCH POP LYRICS, ROUGHLY TRANSLATED FOR MY BENEFIT.

IT IS MY FIRST TIME GETTING THIS SORT OF ATTENTION.

IT FEELS LIKE I'M IN (ANOTHER) BAD MOVIE.

1995 I AM 19.
I AM FRANK-N-FURTER.

PARTLY BECAUSE THE GUY WHO PLAYED FRANK STOPPED SHOWING UP AND I WAS THE ONE WHO KNEW THE LINES AND WAS WILLING TO WEAR THE CORSET.

PARTLY, I THINK, BECAUSE CERTAIN PEOPLE WERE UNDER THE IMPRESSION THAT ME BEING FRANK WOULD GET THEM LAID.

IT WOULD NOT.

SOMEHOW BEING FRANK IS MAKING ME FALL OUT OF LOVE WITH HIM.

MAYBE BECAUSE I'M A WEIRD LOOKING FRANK.

AND STARING AT MYSELF IN THE MIRROR AS I SMEAR ON BLUE, THE CHARACTER SEEMS LESS... SMOLDERING.

MAYBE IT'S BECAUSE I'VE MET MY FIRST DYKES.

DYKES WHO OFFER POETRY AND SEX INSTEAD OF FICTION, WHICH I AM HAPPY TO TAKE THEM UP ON.

SOMETIME BEFORE HALLOWEEN, I SLIP OFF MY $10.99 PUMPS AND RIPPED FISHNETS,

AND LOOK FOR SOMETHING REAL.

Love in the Time of Ethernet: Geeks & LDR

Natalie Zina Walschots

In twelve days, I am moving to Montreal to start a PhD.

There are a lot of reasons that I shouldn't kiss this lovely man in front of me, aside from the fact that I am moving away. Cultivating a friendship with Jairus has been one of the great joys of the past year and a half, and I don't want to do anything to jeopardize that. He's been respectful of my space and my person to the point of being almost courtly in his formality, which makes him hard to read, so I'm not totally sure yet that he feels the same kind of giddy attraction that I do. My other partner and I have only recently opened up our relationship, and while he has been dating someone for a few months, I have been hesitant to leap into anything too quickly.

But, Jairus and I have been watching horror movies all night, slowly shifting closer and closer until our forearms are touching, and then our knees, and then our shoulders, and then with one last shift and sigh we're holding each other. But, sitting across a table from him, talking about RPGs and families and writing, has been one of the brightest spots in a very challenging year. But, I am very good at doing very unwise, very brave things. But, he has the most beautiful eyes I have ever seen.

I hug him goodnight, twelve days before I am moving to Montreal with my partner and our dog, for at least five years and possibly forever. I am standing in his kitchen wearing a *GTA V* hat and a vest with a Carcass patch stitched to the back, in my armour but feeling raw. He is smiling down at me gently as I am about to leave, so I stop. I take off my hat and pause again. I put my hands on his chest and can feel his heart beating so hard, like I am touching the breastbone of some great bird.

I gather my stupid courage together, and I kiss him.

Twelve days later, I load everything I own into a U-Haul and move 542 kms away from his kiss and his kitchen. By then, it's already become clear that something extraordinary has happened. That he's not just a friend that I smooched, that our future isn't vague fondness and the odd night of horror movies and make-outs scattered across the coming months. That whatever the future holds, our stories have dovetailed now, and the narratives moving forward will always be entwined.

Before the summer is over and my classes begin, my other relationship has dissolved and my now-former partner moved back to Toronto. I have gone back to visit Jairus for a weekend and discovered the ardour and affection and genuine magic is only growing. The last weekend of the summer, Jairus and his other partner, Audra, and her other partner, Chris, (darling, wonderful friends of mine already) and I go to a wedding in Quebec City together, stopping by a fairy forest and having many fantastic brunches in the process. By the end of that summer, we are a family.

Suddenly I find myself staring down five years separated from the people I love most in the entire world, who have thrown the doors to my heart wide open. For the foreseeable future, the great love of my life is sleeping five hours away from me. We begin to build a relationship out of the love we have found with a great deal of time and geography in the way.

So, we tackle the problem like geeks.

Jairus and I do massive amounts of research like the unrepentant nerds we are. We find apps and websites to help us, join Reddit groups dedicated to long-distance relationships. Jairus sources the best webcams and headset mics for multi-hour conversations and we order them immediately.

We are already used to flirting with each other via social media and having long conversations via chat; those channels of communication only deepen. We deluge each other's Facebook walls with links and images, tag each other in tweets; he and Audra begin a Pinterest board of sweet and spooky things I might like.

We gleefully discover that the geekiest of our shared interests lend themselves extremely well to long distance relationships. We watch great horror films and bad sci-fi flicks together, chatting via our headsets while we watch our screens in sync, sharing commentary and reactions. We create playlists of ridiculous Youtube videos; sometimes Jairus makes playlists for me, or will host a DJ channel for two so I can listen to music he picks for us while I am doing my class reading for the week.

Playing online co-op videogames becomes an anchor of our time together. We play hours and hours of *Bloodborne*, Hidetaka Miyazaki's opus, leaving poems in beautiful little corners of the gothic nightmare landscape, helping each other with the most terrifying boss battles. He laughs hysterically when I scream and squawk and swear at the worst jump scares. For our first anniversary, I have a portrait made of our *Bloodborne* avatars, celebrating the way we develop ways of fighting together that complement our playing styles: my blunt hack and slash with a saw-cleaver or stake driver, his elegant long-range flourishes with the axe.

We play even more *Destiny.* We wear identical helmets and shaders, so we're a matched pair as we patrol the moon or run strikes, shooting aliens, yelling and cursing and hooting at each other through headsets. I become an administrator for Feminist War Cult and Jairus is one of the first members, and so we carry the proud SJW standard into the more sinister reaches of space.

It's deeply surprising to me, at first, how intimate playing videogames with a romantic partner is; it's something I have never done before. I was always terrified to have someone else watch me play. I barely picked up the controller in previous relationships, preferring to watch, and when I did play in someone else's company it was almost always JRPGs that had little to do with movement or hand-eye coordination. At the Canadian Game Studies Association conference in Ottawa in the Spring, Emma Vossen eloquently discusses how nerve-wracking playing games with a partner can be for women. "At some point I realized that it took more vulnerability on my part to play videogames with men than to have sex with them," she says. "This raised a lot of questions for myself. Why was I more afraid to pick up a controller than take off my clothes?" Becoming comfortable enough to play around Jairus was its own exploration of intimacy.

When my workload becomes too intense for me to carve out an entire evening to hunt down the Blades of Crota or work on a new dungeon, Jairus Twitch streams games while I work. I tune in on my headset, listening to him play *Shovel Knight*, occasionally offering a comment while drafting papers or fixing my citations. We learn how to passively spend time, inhabiting space together gently, each of us in our own city, doing something separate, but still, gently, touching.

Our wildly successful integration of love and geekery solves other problems of distance. In order to participate in social gatherings at Jairus' house, including Audra's and Chris' birthdays, I become a telepresence robot. I stumble on this possibility while Skyping in to play D&D with my group back home, and find they have set me up on a laptop in the DM's living room that is balanced on a stack of books in my usual seat, I was still inhabiting my spot. Jairus tries the experiment the next time a UFC fight is scheduled that we both want to watch. He places a laptop on a chair with a web cam coiled around the back so I have a better vantage of the room; the momentary weirdness of my face on the screen fades quickly, and soon everyone is interacting with me as though I am really there. Later, he sets me up more formally on one of the laptop stands he uses when performing music live, and he begins referring to it as my "legs." In this form I chat with my friends in his house, participate in Value Village fashion shows, watch superhero movies with the people I love.

We get better and better at being geeks in love all the time, distance be damned. After all, we're planning on doing this for the long haul, until I earn a doctorate, so we plan for fully half a decade of living five hours apart from each other. We operate as though this was going to be the way things are for the foreseeable future.

In doing this, we thrive. On the relatively rare occasions we are in the same space, long weekends every few weeks and longer visits at Christmas and Spring Break, we make the time that we have count for everything we can. We go on fantastic dates at ridiculous restaurants and spent nights in eating terrible pizza. We learn how to talk to each other, where each of us was tough and tender, what to poke and what to approach carefully. We share vast amounts of media, telling our story using other people's narratives, the fervency of fandom brought to bear on the love growing between us.

We understand the intimacy of tangled wires, of whispers carried over ethernet. There's no replacing touch, breath, closeness, but there are lots of other things, other ways of loving, and we throw ourselves into them. On days I can't see his face, he sends me selfies; when we can't kiss, I write him stories.

We become very, very good at being in love with each other while we are apart. But, as we get more skilled at being nerds in a wonderful long-distance relationship, it becomes clearer and clearer that neither our nerdery nor our ever-increasing LDR skill sets are making the distance any less excruciating. As we build lives around each other and new habits became flourishing routines, the depth to which I miss him becomes more and more acute. Parting moves from bittersweet to agonizing. The fairytales I write become darker, full of towers and caves and loneliness.

I spend two glorious months in Toronto over the summer, in the same city as my partner and my family. We fall into a different kind of rhythm, of short walks to meet each other for coffee dates, of sweetly casual meetings and painless partings. Time together loses a bit of the edge of scarcity. The joy I have only felt for a few days at a time here and there stretches out and holds for weeks on end.

When the time comes for me to go back to Montreal, the school year threatening to begin any moment, I decide, slowly and then all at once, that I am not returning. That I don't want to. That my life and my heart is here, and that as good as Jairus and I have become at being in love while we are apart, all those tactics and all that practice have only proven to me, beyond a shadow of a doubt, that being close, and being home, is what I am supposed to be doing.

Within two weeks I have moved back. Suddenly four more years of never-ending chat logs and multi-hour Skype calls and dates that include ordering two different pizzas in two different cities while we do Weekly Heroic missions evaporates. A future that was once years away is suddenly here. I can walk to his house in less than half an hour, and instead of calls my calendar is suddenly full of travel plans and work parties and sleepover dates.

Newly transplanted, with whole new ways of being, and being together, to figure out and giddily explore, I can see the lovely, geeky LDR patterns we've established making our IRL relationship even better. We still send each other selfies, even when we're ever only going to be apart for days or hours instead of weeks. We still post links we might like to each other's Facebook walls. We still play hours and hours of *Destiny* together, but now, our PS4s are nestled together on his entertainment unit, a second large monitor next to his television, and we sit side by side, legs tangled, while we shoot aliens together in matching armour.

A FIRST. BY GILLIAN G.

THIS IS THE STORY OF MY FIRST DATE. IT WAS NOT A "GOOD DATE." BUT IT HAD A LOT AGAINST IT FROM THE BEGINNING.

FOR STARTERS, I WAS 18 YEARS OLD.

A LATE-BLOOMING 18 YEAR OLD, EXTRA-VIRGIN.

SO FRESH!

VERY INEXPERIENCED

FOR THE MAIN COURSE, I DIDN'T REALLY LIKE THE GUY.

THIS ONE, I GUESS...

ALSO, HIS DAD WAS THERE. ON THE SIDE.

IT COMES WITH WHAT?!

NO SUBSTITUTIONS.

I FINISHED HIGH SCHOOL WITHOUT EVER HAVING A MALE HUMAN SHOW ANY INTEREST IN ME.

MINT-IN-BOX

UNIVERSITY... WAS GOING TO BE DIFFERENT.

HA HA HA HA HA

AND IT WAS! SUDDENLY MY FRIENDS AND I HUNG OUT WITH GUYS.

AFTER ONE STUDY SESSION I GOT THE WORD:

SOMEONE HAS A CRUSH ON YOU!

WHAT?! WHO?!!

OH

IT'S KURT!

POOF!

CAN HE CALL YOU?

SURE.

AND HE ACTUALLY DID. CALL.

YOU'RE GOOD TO TALK TO!

Hi Gillian, It's KURT.

UH

AND BECAUSE I DIDN'T LIKE-LIKE HIM, I WAS RELAXED ENOUGH TO ACTUALLY TALK TO HIM LIKE A NORMAL PERSON.

THIS WENT ON FOR ABOUT A WEEK, UNTIL...

Want to go to a movie on Friday?

UH

THIS IS WHERE MY INEXPERIENCE STEERED ME VERY, VERY WRONG.

I DON'T REALLY WANT TO BE SEEN OUT WITH THIS GUY.

LET'S WATCH A MOVIE IN INSTEAD

OKAY!

whew
~BOOP

WOO!
CLICK

THIS IS HOW NAIVE I WAS. MY HIGH SCHOOL EXPERIENCE WAS

THIS **NOT** THIS

HANGING IN SUBURBAN "RUMPUS ROOMS" WITH ONLY GIRLS, NOT DRINKING.

COOL TEENS, HIP DRUGS, KEGS, MAKE-OUT PARTIES... I ASSUME?!

SO WHEN I SUGGESTED WE "STAY IN" TO "WATCH A MOVIE" I HAD NO IDEA THAT WHILE I WAS THINKING → THIS

KURT WAS MUCH MORE LIKELY THINKING → THIS

The Panelboard Basement of LUST

AT LEAST UNTIL I SPOKE TO MY BEST FRIEND JAIME:

You told him WHAT?!

WHAT?!

OH.

= ♡♡
XXX!!
*G!

OH NO

SO DID I CANCEL? OR EXPLAIN? OH NO. TOO SCARED TO BE HONEST WITH MYSELF OR ANYONE ELSE...

Our phone chats were OK...

What if I never get asked out again?

...I GOT READY FOR MY FIRST DATE.

1. *Glasses**
2. *Huge Shirt**
3. *Overalls**
4. *Dirty Sneakers**

* SPECIFICALLY CHOSEN TO DETRACT

IT'S DATE NIGHT. TEMPERATURE ¯28°C & SNOWING. PORTENTOUS.

HE PICKS ME UP

I PICK THE MOVIE

CAR WON'T START

WE GET A BOOST

THE BASEMENT (OF "LUST")

WATCHING THE MOVIE

AND DOES HIS **IRONING.**

FINALLY THE DYSTOPIAN FUTURE MOVIE ENDED, RETURNING US TO THE DYSTOPIAN PRESENT.

I GUESS I'll TAKE YOU HOME.

FFT!

YES

♫ Baaaby faaace ♫

baby face
baby face

QUIVERING WITH DESIRE TO BE ANYWHERE ELSE

THE SECOND THE CAR STOPPED:

BYE.

SLAM

?!

I HAD The ICK: I WAS SHAKEN UP, GROSSED OUT, WEIRDED UP & FURIOUS — MOSTLY WITH MYSELF. FOR GETTING INTO THIS, BUT ALSO FOR NOT GETTING MYSELF OUT. FOR FREEZING UP WHEN I COULD HAVE SPOKEN. SAID ANYTHING. KURT WAS FINE, ACTUALLY. I WAS THE PROBLEM.

HOW DID THIS EVEN HAPPEN?

I KNOW, BUT IT WAS THE WORST!

YOU GUYS SPOONED? THAT'S IT?

AW! THAT SUCKS.

THANKS.

SO STARTING THAT DAY (AND FOR THE NEXT 2 YEARS) I WENT BACK TO WHAT I KNEW: FRIENDSHIP.

THERE'S NOTHING LIKE RE-HASHING A BAD DATE UNDER A KITCHEN TABLE WITH YOUR BEST FRIEND (WHO IS SPOONING YOU TO WASH LAST NIGHT'S ICKY SPOON AWAY).

EPILOGUE: NEITHER KURT NOR I EVER CALLED EACH OTHER AGAIN.

The Vulcan in Me

Emma Woolley

SPOCK (convincing himself): *I am in control of my emotions.*
– "The Naked Time"

The first time I really noticed Spock, he was playing chess with Kirk. The episode was, of course, "Where No Man Has Gone Before," the official pilot for *Star Trek: The Original Series*. I was watching it many decades after it aired – mostly out of boredom with a bit of curiosity. I enjoyed space stories and science fiction in general, and thought: Who's the hot pointy-eared guy who can rock better eye makeup than me? This scene is an excellent introduction to the camaraderie and banter between Spock and Kirk:

> **SPOCK:** *I'll have you checkmated your next move.*
> **KIRK:** *Have I ever mentioned you play a very irritating game of chess, Mister Spock?*
> **SPOCK:** *Irritating? Ah, yes. One of your Earth emotions.*
> *(Kirk checkmates Spock, who raises an eyebrow.)*
> **KIRK:** *Certain you don't know what irritation is?*
> **SPOCK:** *The fact that one of my ancestors married a human female...*
> **KIRK:** *Terrible, having bad blood like that.*

Kirk is being cheeky, obviously – but he's also touching on a core part of Spock's character: his constant struggle to submerge his human (and therefore potentially emotional) side. To borrow one of his favourite descriptors, I found this fascinating. What was it like, I wondered, to live without the unpredictability, the ups and downs, the raw wildness of feeling?

See, I'm an emotional person. We all are to varying degrees, but I'm out there with my emotions. When I care about things, I really care about them. I am someone who cries when something bad happens to her favourite imaginary characters, or simply whenever they cry (looking at you, Whedon). In other words, I am what some might refer to as "sensitive" and what a lot of people likely consider "too sensitive" (I prefer "woman of great passions," alas).

The best way to describe my inner world is to not really try. Emotions, often past ones, surface quickly and sometimes unpredictably. They're like surprise jolts of electricity, catching me off-guard and demanding my full attention. Decision-making turns my brain inside out because I spend days researching and cramming information into it – only to end up choosing "what feels right" anyway because I'm so overwhelmed.

Spock, though, is spared these troubles (or so I thought). He doesn't think about emotions and he makes decisions in mere seconds! I bet his mom never encouraged him to "grow a thicker skin."

It made sense that I was drawn to him. The more Star Trek I watched, the more intense my crush became. It's now common for lovers and friends to gift me with Spock-related items for my ever-expanding collection. Spock came to represent both an attraction and a promise of the kind of person I could perhaps become, given time, practice, and maybe a few mind-melds.

My favourite, very silly Spock-related pastime is imagining our potential compatibility, physical and otherwise. I have no doubts about our sexual connection. The fact that Spock is half Vulcan and half-human assures me that he would know much about how our physiology could connect and would generally have some skills. It's only logical. But would I be endlessly frustrated by his inability to show emotion?

ME: I just want you to tell me what you're feeling.
SPOCK: What I am feeling is irrelevant.

ME: Not to me!

SPOCK: You are human; so that is your nature, not mine. Your request is illogical.

ME: *eyes roll out of head*

But hey, if Sarek and Amanda made it work, so could we, right?

Sex and demanding feelings talk aside, I admired Vulcan culture. No war or petty motives for violence; freedom from troubling feelings and overwhelming sadness; babes like Spock. What wasn't to like? The only issue was that I was only seeing what I wanted to see: the absence of emotion.

> **KIRK:** *Er, Mister Spock, when you're finished, please come back and see me. I want to talk to you. This regrettable tendency you've been showing lately towards flagrant emotionalism.*
> **SPOCK:** *I see no reason to insult me, sir. I believe I've been completely logical about the whole affair.*
> — *"The Menagerie, Part 2"*

Vulcans aren't alone in painting emotions with one big, black "terrible" brush. Most humans are not only emotionally inept, but outwardly condemn having feelings. Try typing, "emotions are" into a Google box. For me, the top three suggested phrases were completed with: "irrational," "for the weak," and "useless." This is obviously not a scientifically sound experiment, but I'd argue that these results reflect how a lot of people feel about emotion.

The Original Series often explored tensions between emotion and logic, ultimately arguing that both are required to truly live and evolve. The Vulcans opted to suppress all emotion, considering it an unnecessary setback for their people. Their primary mistake, as I'm sure others will agree, was attempting to separate the two.

Today, we know that logic and emotion are not necessarily enemies or opposites. Before our more logical chunks of brain evolved, we survived entirely with intuition, instinct and emotion. Appraisal theory says that emotions are the result of our assessments of situations. If our emotions are inappropriate it is not because of them, but because of the cognitive framework underpinning them. In other words:

emotions are entirely logical, it is sometimes our reasoning that is off and needs some tinkering. That is, of course, a pretty basic summary of a complicated process – emotion and reason are always working together, along with external factors; and I haven't even addressed motivations – but I think you get the idea.

I think much of Northwestern society is scared of emotion. This is especially true amongst us white people, who embraced positivism and said "nope" to feelings (any WASPs in the house? You know what I'm talking about). We simply don't get in touch with them, listen to them, or figure out what's really going on.

Then there's the whole "women are naturally emotional and therefore weak" belief that seems to be, well, everywhere. Femininity has been lumped together with spiritual and emotional parts of humanity for ages, which wouldn't be a big deal if we didn't think of it in such a binary and devalued way. Men and boys are chastised for crying or expressing vulnerability (called "bitches" or "pussies"); while women are expected to be emotional, but only under certain circumstances. Step outside the lines and we might be called "crazy". (Hey, remember when hysteria was a real diagnosis that doctors gave to women who dared protest too much, or had too many feelings?) Our emotions are often used to dismiss us ("Are you on your period or something?") or cast us aside altogether ("Women are irrational"). The difficult question for me, in my experience, has been: How can I really express and be myself while also being taken seriously? At times, this is a real Kobayashi Maru.

It's no wonder so many women try to distance themselves from emotions. I know I wanted to purge myself of the stuff.

SPOCK: *Emotions are alien to me. I'm a scientist.*
LEILA: *Someone else might believe that. Your shipmates, your Captain, but not me. Come.*

– "This Side of Paradise"

My *Star Trek* watching reached a critical level under the best circumstances possible: a breakup. (Also my *Buffy the Vampire Slayer* watching, but that is a whole other essay. Am I the only person who watches a lot of TV when I'm sad?) Anyway, I was a bit of a wreck. I'd just moved to Toronto from a smaller city the year prior, switched career programs, and moved into a new apartment alone.

As if those weren't enough changes to send me spiraling into sadness, I had just been through a painful, unexpected, but necessary break-up. Combine all this with a tendency towards general imbalance and mental health stuff and well, I was feeling very low.

I didn't have many friends or a solid support network, but I did have wine, The Enterprise and my beloved Spock. He would show me the way. I longed to absorb his Vulcan ability to not be affected by hangovers, but more importantly, to dismiss emotion and move on. Yet the more I watched, I realized how wrong I'd been about him.

To the casual Trekkie (or McCoy), Spock is seen as little more than a robot. This is understandable. Spock frequently equates emotions with weakness, denies having them at all, and is flattered when he is compared to a computer. Spock cherishes his Vulcan heritage and tends to think of his human side as a disadvantage. But this does not mean that he doesn't have emotions.

It takes enduring the campy hits and misses of *The Original Series* to see that Spock is a character of extreme duality; he does feel deeply – his struggle is to control and conceal this fact. The most powerful scenes in the series feature Spock facing his emotions by way of some kind of alien interference or time travel: his breakdown over never being able to tell his mother he loved her ("The Naked Time"); his compassion for Captain Pike motivating him to outright mutiny ("The Menagerie, parts 1 and 2"); the way he wiped away Leila's tears once she realized he wouldn't stay with her after a carefree romp on a planet ("You couldn't pronounce it," my heart! – "This Side of Paradise"); how he let himself be deceived by Zarabeth because he wanted to stay in an ice age with her ("All Our Yesterdays"). You'd have to be an actual robot to not be moved, or see just how much love Spock holds under his calm and collected exterior.

My crush was almost jeopardized. Opposites attracted no longer. Spock and I had something very real in common: the struggle for control and balance. Our external selves were quite polarized – he needed to make peace with the human in him, and I needed to find the Vulcan in me – but not at the expense of other parts of us. I reflected on how strangely I had been acting: getting into dead-end dating situations, refusing to be vulnerable, treating people poorly, drinking way too much, contemplating how to disappear. I had finally reached a point where I didn't feel very much at all and it wasn't as satisfying as I had imagined. As Spock eventually learned, the solution was never to become so tough and rigid that I can't feel at all, but to accept that I can.

> **SPOCK:** *Being split in two halves is no theory with me, Doctor. I have a human half, you see, as well as an alien half, submerged, constantly at war with each other. Personal experience, Doctor. I survive it because my intelligence wins out over both, makes them live together.*
>
> *– "The Enemy Within"*

Part of being a very emotional person means I am always collecting mementos – often in the form of tattoos. I get images I want to remember, or messages that I can't let myself forget. So, shortly after Nimoy's death – probably the only celebrity passing that has ever devastated me – I found myself on a stool in a Toronto tattoo parlour, watching a stone-faced guy tattoo "LLAP" inside the outline of a heart on my right wrist.

I'm sure it seems like some really cheesy nerd tattoo I picked off some artist's quickie board. To me, it's something else entirely. It isn't just a memorial to the extraordinary man who brought tremendous warmth and gravitas to a character that could have easily been the laughing stock of the franchise. It is also a reminder to hold both parts of myself together with equal amounts of pride; that the secret to living well and prospering is to open oneself up to emotion. And every time I look at it, it feels pretty damn good.

Better Than Fiction

Ever since I felt my first butterflies, relationships between fictional characters were the central outlet for my own blossoming feelings and sexuality.

Fiction

By Sarah Winifred Searle

Inspired by this, I started writing and drawing my own romances.

I was okay at it.

Eventually, people even started paying me to create these stories.

But I had a *deep, dark secret...*

I didn't believe in love.
Not in that sense, anyway.

Not for myself.

I had relationships, sure. And it would be unfair to say that they didn't mean something.

But my experiences felt lukewarm in comparison to the deep, sincere, gratuitous layers of meaning that can be crafted into a good story.

I resigned myself to mediocrity.

Sometimes I wondered if I was broken.

But that was okay. If I needed romance in my life, I'd create it.

When writing and drawing became my job, I sought a way to keep my creative spark.

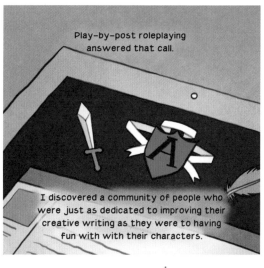

Play-by-post roleplaying answered that call.

I discovered a community of people who were just as dedicated to improving their creative writing as they were to having fun with with their characters.

We wove quests and battles into epics, forging lasting friendships along the way -- both in character, and out.

I learned how to write truly great characters, some of which became so real that they developed wills of their own.

One of them even dared to fall in love.

It made sense. They had helped each other through harrowing trials, forming a bond like no other.

They complemented each other: one bold, one cautious.

Both strong.

Both flawed.

Meanwhile, I grew closer to the other character's writer.

We had already been friends for years.

I respected him immensely as a writer, and he proofread my professional scripts.

STRESSED!

DAVID

BELIEVE IN YOURSELF

He offered invaluable emotional support as I worked toward realizing my dreams as a cartoonist.

And despite our twelve hour time difference, when we wrote together, we had *so much fun.*

It happened so easily.

THANKS FOR THAT FEEDBACK, I DON'T KNOW WHAT I'D DO WITHOUT YOU.

We were doomed from the start.

...uh oh

It was my very own, perfectly suited, couldn't-have-written-it-better-myself meet-cute.

Falling for him made complete sense. But he was all the way in Australia, and being so invested in another person *terrified* me. So, of course, I agonized over it...

Then he flew across the world so we could be together for real, and it was everything I'd dreamed.

I'd lost hope that I could feel that way without sacrificing my passion, but the person worth loving wasn't just someone cute who was nice to me.

He was the person who could truly inspire me to reach my potential for my *first* love: storytelling.

And you know, just for the record...

He's *far* better than fiction.

Popping the Heat Sink

When Videogame Love Becomes True Love

Sam Maggs, illustration by Selena Goulding

Fellow *Secret Loves of Geek Girls* contributor Soha Kareem and I used to hate each other, and for the worst reason. Oh, you know it: a *boy*. I had spent some time dating this one complete jerk, and after we broke up, Soha spent some time dating that *same* complete jerk. We all shared a few classes together, pretending not to notice each other from across the room, and *definitely* not staring daggers at each other's backs while pretending to take notes. It wasn't until after we were both well free of him, that – while creeping Soha's Twitter, of course – I noticed *her* subtweeting about *me, too.* Realizing that half of the reason I had been so obsessed with her is because she seemed *so cool and smart and awesome, dammit,* I reached out to her to be like, why are we spending our time hating *each other* when we could be spending our time *together* hating *this complete jerk* instead?

And thus, a beautiful, life-long friendship was born. Now I love her like she was my own sister – and all because of a shared ex.

Strange as it may sound, I think a similar sort of foundation is the fundamental tenet of fan communities. You bond with other people online or IRL over your shared love – or, sometimes, hatred – for something; be it the fifth season of new *Doctor Who* (love, obviously), or the lack of a *Black Widow* solo film (super extra mega hate, but that's a story for a different essay). But, while fandom friendships are inarguably incredible, there is something so strong, so specific, about bonding over *someone else*, be it a mutual friend or frenemy, that tends to form the most intense friendships, even if we don't want to admit it.

Which brings me to Alistair Theirin.

I was twenty-four when I first met Alistair. Not at a bar, or in class, or even at a pretentious coffee shop like the one in which I wrote this essay, but – in the tradition of most successful romantic comedies – in the first hour or so of *Dragon Age: Origins*. I later read that he was specifically written to be a perfect mixture of Xander from *Buffy the Vampire Slayer* and Malcolm Reynolds from *Firefly* so – being the Joss Whedon apologist that I am – I was doomed from the start. This wasn't my first experience with a memorable fantasy RPG character (no, that would be Minsc from *Baldur's Gate*); nor was it my first time finding myself, awkwardly and despite my own best intentions, falling into a very particular half-love half-obsession with a fictional human (that honor undoubtedly goes to Numair Salmalín, from Tamora Pierce's *The Immortals* quartet). This *was*, however, the first time that the media I was consuming actively encouraged me to pursue a romantic relationship with said character. Blame it on the woeful lack of JRPGs in my formative gaming education, but romancing someone *in a game* was suddenly the realest thing ever. When my Warden was flirting with Alistair and getting flustered, shy responses in return, *I too* was suffering through those same emotions. When our weird, hexagonally-rendered bodies got down, I was feelin' it (thanks in part to some supplemental fanfiction, of course); when we were faced with death, I let him bang my caustic witchy friend to save his life. I replayed the entire game as a human lady just so we could get married. I was in deep.

Thus began a long and storied tradition of falling for characters from BioWare games. After Alistair came raucous, riled-up pirate princess Isabela in *Dragon Age II*, followed by the Iron Bull in *Dragon Age: Inquisition* (a pansexual horned half-dragon with a penchant for BDSM, naturally). These emotional entanglements were all surpassed by my three-game One True Videogame Love, the *Mass Effect* trilogy's Garrus Vakarian, a bird/dinosaur alien sharpshooter with a vengeance complex. I don't think I'll ever fully dig myself out of that hole, if I'm being honest with myself.

As you might imagine, finding myself hopelessly in love with a bunch of fictional videogame characters was not only detrimental to my self-esteem (*what am I doing with my life, who am I, what's wrong with me, what have I done,* etc.), but also to my IRL romantic relationships. When I was single, I was measuring all potential partners up against my meticulously-crafted digital babes: Alistair's well-written charms; Isabela's witty banter, edited to perfection; Garrus's computer-modulated yet uncomfortably-attractive voice (seriously, *what is wrong with me?*) Once I managed to stumble my way into a long-term relationship, my partner was very generously okay with the preposterous number of hours I spent romancing these fake people instead of, you know, him.

But while I was probably destroying my chances at ever having a healthy and normal romantic relationship ever again (*whoops!*), I wasn't sure what effect – if any – it was going to have on my friendships. Mostly I just didn't tell anyone about my weirdly all-consuming new obsessions; my best friend is a lawyer without so much as a Wii to her name – she was going to have *no* idea what I was talking about, let alone be able to identify or sympathize with me about my now full-time heartache. Even texting any of my comic book or television-obsessed friends with "Hey, let's talk about my videogame relationships" seemed inadvisable. Instead, I did what all well-adjusted adults with a – uh, "nontraditional" – relationship with a fictional character eventually do: I turned to the Internet.

It's a fandom story as old as time (or, at least, dial-up): you love something; you feel isolated; you go online; you discover there are thousands of other people who love that something just as much as you do; you get all warm and fuzzy and accepty all over the place. But *this* time I wasn't content to lurk about as usual; I had so many feels that I just *had* to talk about them *somewhere* or I was absolutely going to *explode.* Shouting frantically about my videogame heartache into what felt like the empty void of social media was cathartic in and of itself – but when ladies started responding to me in droves, I knew something magical was happening.

Suddenly, I knew tons of other gals who'd had their hearts broken and trampled on by the same men and women; ladies who'd been on the exact same emotional roller coasters; who'd also felt a little strange about the whole thing but had ultimately come to accept this part of their lives. I shared exes with *all of them*. We were instant friends, connected by the universal experience of having loved the same someone – even if that someone was, admittedly, digital.

At first, I wasn't entirely sure how to navigate these relationships; was it weird to share my favorite NC-17 fanfic with my new friends? What about that epic shirtless fanart that made me all sweaty? Was that crossing a line? Well, *maybe*; but ultimately, pushing past that boundary just brought us all that much closer together. The self-awareness that allowed us to recognize how ridiculous our obsessions were also let us be less uptight around each other; the conversational restrictions you might place on a *regular* burgeoning friendship just didn't seem to exist when you know that you're all just a little bit more "out there" than usual. They understood when I DM'd them in tears about a difficult relationship moment during a replay; they sympathized when I told them I was exhausted because I'd stayed up until 4 am the previous night reading a sixty-chapter post-*Mass Effect 3* happily-ever-after fic; they talked me through my feelings that time I became legitimately distraught over the fact that I would never, tragically, be part of a romantic rag-tag spaceship crew. They knew everything I was going through because they'd been there themselves, many times. They were perfect for me.

Before I knew it, I had an amazing network of awesome lady friends online, brought together by this odd shared dating experience; we were mailing each other game-related gifts, and getting matching tattoos, and rooming together at conventions. In the most unexpected way, I *had* found love through videogames – the love of these awesome gals, accomplished and interesting and BioWare trash; women with whom I'm proud to have such close relationships.

And that makes all the in-game heartache completely, totally worth it.

Biographies

FIONNA ADAMS
writer, "Pop Culture Metaphor"
Fionna Adams is a fat, poly, queer, intersex trans girl from New York who writes comics. **Twitter: @letao_nox**

ALB
cartoonist, "Settings"
ALB is a tiny illustrator living in Toronto. She made her debut with *Flight*, a comic about long distance relationships.
Twitter: @albinwonderland

SANYA ANWAR
illustrator
Sanya Anwar is a Toronto based illustrator and comic creator.

JEN APRAHAMIAN
writer & illustrator, "Read 1:19 am"
Jen Aprahamian is a writer and technology entrepreneur who splits time between Los Angeles and San Francisco. **Twitter: @jennifermarie**

MARGARET ATWOOD
cartoonist, "Comics, Paper Dolls, Glasses, Contacts"
Margaret Atwood is a writer of novels and so forth who also draws comics.

JEN BARTEL
illustrator
Jen Bartel is a Minneapolis-based illustrator and comic artist who is well known for her ongoing covers on *Jem and the Holograms*.

JORDIE BELLAIRE
colourist, "Dibs on the Goblin King"
Jordie Bellaire is an American Eisner Award-winning colorist living in Ireland with her Irish cat Buffy.

MARGUERITE BENNETT
writer, "Minas Tirith"
Marguerite Bennett lives in Los Angeles, and has worked for DC Comics, Marvel, and BOOM.

JORDYN BOCHON
colours, "Pining Over Puzzled Pints"
Jordyn F Bochon lives by the sea and makes spooky comics in pastel colors.

MEAGHAN CARTER
cartoonist, "Mechanism"
Meaghan is a Toronto-based comic artist, author of webcomics *Take off!* and *Godslave*.

ALICIA CONTESTABILE
writer, "Never Kiss a Writer"
Alicia Contestabile is a writer and game designer. **Twitter: @swizzle_kiss**

STEPHANIE COOKE
writer, "Lungerella"
Stephanie is a writer, editor and podcaster for *Talking Comics* and *The Missfits.*. **Twitter: @hellocookie**

DANIELLE CORSETTO
cartoonist, "Girls With Slingshots"
Danielle Corsetto is the creator of Girls With Slingshots (and several other, smaller comics projects) girlswithslingshots.com

ERIN COSSAR
writer, "Anne of LINUX PINE"
Erin Cossar is an artist, writer, graphic designer, and book fiend.
Twitter: coss_TO

BRANDY DAWLEY
writer, "Heard it on the Grapevine", "A Different Kind of Fantasy Roleplay"
Brandy is a writer, segment producer, and president of an all-woman's combat sports league.

LESLIE ANN DOYLE
illustrator, "A Different Kind of Fantasy Roleplay"
Leslie Doyle is a freelance illustrator, wife, mother of two, karaoke star, and geek. **Twitter: @AngelCreations**

CARA ELLISON
writer, "The Control Systems of Desire"
Cara Ellison is a game narrative designer who used to ply a trade as a critic but now makes games full time. **Twitter: @caraellison**

MEAGS FITZGERALD
cartoonist, "Waxing Moon"
Meags Fitzgerald is a Montreal-based illustrator and the author of the award-winning *Photobooth: A Biography* and *Long Red Hair*.

J.M. FREY
writer, "How Fanfiction Made Me Gay"
J.M. Frey is a voice actor, award-winning SF/F author, fanthropologist, and professional smartypants.
Twitter: @scifrey

GILLIAN G.
cartoonist, "A First"
Gillian G. is a Toronto-based cartoonist and illustrator, who writes and draws the webcomic jerkfaceahole.com and co-founded Drunk Feminist Films.
Twitter: @GillianGDotCom

SELENA GOULDING
illustrator, "Popping the Heat Sink"
Selena Goulding illustrates comics and stuff and spends most of her free time gaming.

ROBERTA GREGORY
cartoonist, "Bemused"
Roberta Gregory, who lives in Seattle, has been writing and drawing comics since the 1960s and is best known for the notorious Bitchy Bitch.

KRISTEN GUDSNUK
illustrator, various stories
Kristen Gudsnuk is a New York City-based comic artist and writer. She is the creator of *Henchgirl*.
Twitter: @henchgirl_comic

JANET HETHERINGTON
writer & illlustrator, "Both Sides of the Table and Between the Sheets"
Janet Hetherington spends way too much time reading comic books and watching TV and movies, but it's okay because she creates that stuff too. #ilovemyjob **Twitter: @bestdestiny**

CHERELLE HIGGINS
writer, "Cherry"
Cherelle Higgins is a full-time cat-wrangling weirdo, part-time filmmaker. Calls Toronto home and likes to lift all the things at the gym
Twitter: @Cherelleski

TINI HOWARD
writer, "Fanfiction, F/F, Angst"
Tini Howard is a writer of and about comics, mostly.
Twitter: @tinihoward.

GITA JACKSON
writer, "URL>IRL"
Gita Jackson is a writer, assistant editor of Paste Magazine, and podcaster on Match 3.

LORETTA JEAN
writer, "Levelling Up Your Dating Profile"
Loretta Jean identifies as a queer and poly glamourwitch, academic, burlesque performer and producer. She resides in Toronto.
Twitter: @loretta_jean

SOHA KAREEM
writer, "Mashing Our Buttons"
Soha Kareem is a ex-academic and experimental artist who loves glitch photography, *Supernatural*, *Mass Effect*, and *Fallout*.

MELISSA KAY
illustrator, "No Country for Old Mentors"
Melissa Kay is a biomedical illustrator by day and a kung fu assassin by night. She resides in Texas.
Twitter: @mechamelissa

MEGAN KEARNEY
cartoonist, "Regards to the Goblin King", "Yes, No, Maybe"

Megan Kearney is a Toronto-based cartoonist and manager of Comic Book Embassy. She teaches character design at an animation college.
Twitter: @spookymeggie

IRENE KOH
cartoonist, "Nerd Love"

Irene Koh is an illustrator based out of LA. She is also a judoka, aspiring polyglot, and foie gras enthusiast.
Twitter: @kohquette

ADRIENNE KRESS
writer, "I'm Your Biggest Fan"

Adrienne Kress is a Toronto-based author, actor, playwright, screenwriter, director, producer, cinephile, and a fan of commas. **Twitter: @AdrienneKress**

GISÈLE LAGACÉ
cover artist, Cartoonist "MA3 & Sticky Dilly Buns"

Gisèle Lagacé is a Canadian comic artist whose work includes pencilling for Archie Comics, and creating her own comics at PixieTrixComix.

MEGAN LAVEY-HEATON
book design, writer "How Fanfiction from an American Girl Captured an English Boy"

Megan Lavey-Heaton is the co-creator of *Namesake*. She requires two books at her fingertips, her sonic screwdriver, and a cat on her arm. **Twitter: @savvyliterate**

SAM MAGGS
writer, "Popping the Heat Sink"

Sam Maggs is the bestselling author of *The Fangirl's Guide to the Galaxy* from Quirk Books. **Twitter: @SamMaggs**

DIANA MCCALLUM
writer, "4 Fictional Happy Endings", "There's Nothing Wrong, It Must be Love"

Diana McCallum is a comedy writer, sugar addict, and co-creator of the webcomic *Texts From Superheroes*.
Twitter: @WordsOfDiana

ISABELLE MELANÇON
illustrator, "How Fanfic from an American Girl Captured an English Boy"

Isabelle Melançon is the French Canadian co-creator of Namesake, and co-administrator of Hiveworks.
Twitter: @secondlina.

ANNIE MOK
writer & artist – "Ghost Stories"

Annie Mok is an author-illustrator and a regular contributor to Rookie Mag and The Comics Journal.
Twitter: @HeyAnnieMok

RENEE NAULT
illustrator

Renee Nault lives in Victoria BC, works in watercolour, and is the illustrator of 'The Handmaid's Tale' and 'Witchling'.

LAURA NEUBERT
cartoonist, "They Bury You in White"

Laura Neubert's goal in life is to tell memorable stories and keep creating as long as she is able to.

HOPE NICHOLSON
editor, writer "Rise of the Late Bloomer"

Hope Nicholson is a researcher based out of Toronto who publishes comic books out of her company Bedside Press. **Twitter: @hopelnicholson**

DIANA NOCK
cartoonist, "None the Wiser"

Diana lives in Minneapolis, where she makes a living working for Hiveworks and Slipshine and even gets to draw comics sometimes.
diananock.com **Twitter: @jinxville**

JESS OLIVER-PROULX
writer, "Giant-Sized Regrets"

Jess Oliver Proulx is a web developer and Founding Partner of Nerd North Media & GEEKPRON.com

DEENA PAGLIARELLO
illustrator, "Lungerella"

Deena Pagliarello is an illustrator in Toronto. She loves comics, movies, tea, and naps with her cats and her ever-loving Dan. **Twitter: @deenadraws**

JESSICA PAOLI
illustrator, "Why My Partner is Really a Superhero"

Jessica Paoli is a multidisciplinary designer and illustrator. She wants to bake cookies with you.
Twitter: @skullface

TRINA ROBBINS
writer, "Why My Partner Is Really a Superhero", Foreword

Trina Robbins has been writing comics, graphic novels, and histories of women cartoonists for over 40 years.

SORAYA ROBERTS
writer, "No Country for Old Mentors"

Soraya Roberts is a writer in Toronto working on a book about "My So-Called Life" and a memoir about the journalism industry.
Twitter: @sorayaroberts

SARAH WINIFRED SEARLE
cartoonist, "Better Than Fiction"

Sarah Winifred Searle hails from New England, where she pets cats and makes comics inspired by intimacy.
Twitter: @swinsea

SHOURI
colours, cover, "MA3 & Sticky Dilly Buns"

Ma. Victoria Robado (Shouri) is a comic artist and graphic designer from Argentina. **Twitter: @shourimajo.**

CRYSTAL SKILLMAN
writer, "A Geek Girl of Your Own"

Crystal Skillman is an award-winning playwright. Her home with Fred is indeed filled with comics and plays (and cats!)

NATALIE SMITH
cartoonist, "Kids These Days"

Natalie Smith is a high school student and aspiring artist who spends her time sharing new stories.
Twitter: @comicsaquarius

FIONA SMYTH
artist, "Montreal, 1993"

Fiona Smyth collaborated with Cory Silverberg on the picture book *What Makes A Baby* and the follow up *Sex Is A Funny Word*.

TWIGGY TALLANT
writer, "May I Admire You Again Today?"

Twiggy Tallant is a mechanic stripper wizard, one of a kind collectible, with an addiction to dirt, glamour, black magic, and gasoline from Toronto.

MARIKO TAMAKI
writer, "Montreal, 1993"

Mariko Tamaki's work includes This One Summer and Skim (with Jillian Tamaki). **Twitter: @marikotamaki**

JEN VAUGHN
cartoonist, "Puzzled Over Pints". Artist, "Pop Culture Metaphor"

Jen Vaughn cranks out comics for Cartozia Tales, colors the sexy Archie series and draws Avery Fatbottom. **Twitter: @thejenya**

NATALIE ZINA WALSCHOTS
writer, "Love in the Time of Ethernet"

Natalie Zina Walschots writes about heavy metal, videogames, speculative fiction, S&M, CanLit, combat sports and feminism in Toronto.

RACHAEL WELLS
illustrator, "Cherry"

Rachael Wells is a Toronto-based illustrator/sequential artist. From time to time, she dresses up in a superhero costume & runs a marathon.

KATIE WEST
writer, "A Divorcee's Guide to the Apocalypse"

Katie West is a Canadian cat lady Trekkie living in the UK and currently working as a virtual personal assistant to creatives. **Twitter: @katiewest**

JENN WOODALL
cartoonist, "Shipping"

Jenn Woodall is an illustrator and comics creator from Toronto.
Twitter: @jenn_woodall

EMMA WOOLLEY
writer, "The Vulcan in Me"

Emma Woolley is a writer, proud SJW, and RPG lover currently in social work academia in Toronto.
Twitter: @emmamwoolley

Kickstarter Funders

These Kickstarter backers helped make "Secret Loves of Geek Girls" happen!

@actionGeologist
@dadbodhishattva
@LitLoves
@lly L.
@michdevilish
@s0delightful
@superdumb
@Torvos
☆*Jane*☆
A Godfrey
A McNelis
A silent chap
A. Gladwin
A. Waning
A. Wood
A.G.
A.Miura
Aaron P. Churchill
Abby Dinges
Abby Franquemont
Adam "HWB" Harris
Adam Bishop
Adam Borgeson &
    Karen Fenech
Adam Hines
Adam Miller
Adam Whitcomb
Adriane Hughes Ruzak
Adrienne BP
Agnès Léguillon
Ainslie
Aja Martinez
Alana
Alana Stern
Alanna Gail Kibbe
Alanna Graves
Alden Franklin
Aleandro P.
Alesia & Babs
Alex
Alex
Alex Davies
Alex Bond
Alex H
Alex Robinson
Alexa Dickman
Alexander Tuttle
Alexandra S.
Alexis Petree
Ali Colluccio
Ali Grotkowski
Alicia Acampora
Alicia Mundinger
Aliénor D'Héraby
Alisha Jade
Alisha Walton
Alissa Bourbonnais
Allie Strelbisky
Allison Huffman
Allison O'Toole
Ally H.
Alyssa Rance
Amanda & Oliver
Amanda Barnett
Amanda Brandt
Amanda Brasher
Amanda Clare Lees
Amanda LeFranc
Amanda R Robinson
Amanda Siakel

Amanda V.
Amarin Astarte
Amber Beitzel
Amber Desadier
Amber Garza
Amber Kober
Amber Leedham
Amber Remeeus
    McKibbin
Amber Smith
Amberlee Hanson
Amberly Lorenz
Amelia & Eleanor
    Mason
Amelia Paxman
Amy Makice
Amy N Diegelman
Amy Shier
Amy Tomlinson
Amy VanTorre
Anais Mathers
Anastacia Strate
Andrea Bellemare
Andrea Demonakos
Andrea F.
Andrea Medaris
Andrea Villa
Andreas Fuchs
Andres
Andrew Dmytrasz
Andrew Ferguson
Andrew Ferris
Andrew (Geek Hard)
Andrew Guerr
Andrew Pepoy
Andrew Quodling
Andrew Walsh
Andrew Wilson
Andrey Goder
Andria
Andy Law
Andy Purkiss
Angel Cruz
Angeline Burton
Angharad Lodwick
Ann Doehring
Ann T.
Anna Bradley
Anna Kay
Anna Parikka
Anna Vinter
Anne Brown
Anne Farmer
Anne-Marie J
Anonymous
anterobot
Anthony C Mackaronis
Anthony McColgan
Anthony Nguyen
Antoine Bouthors
Anzan Hoshin
Apostolos Kalantzis
April Nance
aradia
Arianna Iliff
Arianne Hartsell-
    Gundy
Armond Netherly
Ashes Davis
Ashley Black

Ashley Fisher
Ashley Hasna
Ashley Hisson
Ashley McGregor Dey
Ashley Robinson
Ashley Victoria
    Robinson
AshleyRose Bailey
Aubrey Allyn aka Aubs
Audrey Henderson
Audrey St-Arneauld
Austen Marie
Autumn Williams
Ava Leung
Avram Gottschlich
Azrael's Mom
B Small
B. Anderson
B. MacLeod
Backer
Backer
Bae Nam-gyu
Bailey Poland
Barbara Bownds
Barbara Jane Hungate
Barrie D Hardwick
Becca Fronczak
Becca Reighard
Becca Sexton
Becca Shea
Becky McKercher
Bee Quesada
Belinda Morris
Ben Blanchard
Ben Hudson
Ben Kroll
Ben McCabe
Benjamin "Zero"
    Scheyer
Bertha Mason Sandy
Bess Browning
bethae
Betsy
Betsy Deuman
Bianca C.
Blair Mueller
Blair Smith
Blanca Torres-Olave
bmac
Bo Moore
Bobby Shortle
Bonnie Van Toen
Bookkiitten Silvia
Brad Abraham
Brandi Elizabeth
    Brown
Brandy Heinrich
Brenda Marie
Brenna S
Brent Sieling
Brett Brennan
Bri Rudd
Brian "Dub" Alvarez
Brian Berling
Brian Vallee
Brianne Bilyeu
Brianne Nord-Stewart
Britany Arpége Van
    Blake
Brittany Cali

Brittany Helms
Brooke Decker
Brookie Butler
Brookie Judge
Bruce LeCompte
Bryan Wade
Buffy Key
C de B
C Pickersgill
C. E. Emmer
C. Webb
C. Franks
C.N. Rowen
Caitlin B
Caitlin Crossley
Caitlin Howard
Caitlin Regan
Caitlin Rosberg
Caitlin Stary
Caitlyn McKinney
Caitlynn Fairbarns
Caldak
Candi Norwood
CandidGamera
Carl Rigney
Carley Parker
Carlos AGP
Carly A. Kocurek
Carly B
Carly Bornstein
Carmiac
Carol Klio Burrell
Carol Shedd
Caroline Gaston
Caroline Ricard
Caroline Sinders
Carrie Ann Schulze
Carrie Gillon
Casey L. Walker
Casey Rae
Cassandra Brooks
Cassandra Mercer
Cassidy Avery
Cassilynn Brown
Cat A.
Cat Davidson-Hall
Caterina Rindi
Catherine Braiding
Catherine Dolan
Catherine Perlich
CatherineHG
Cathy Razim & Joe
    Pietruch
Cathy Sullivan
Celena Kopinski
Celeste D. Maisel
Chance Davis
Chandra Jessee
Charlene K.
    Humpherys
Chase Vigar
Chasym
Chelsea Holt
Chelsea Hostetter
Chelsea Lyver
Chelsea Slevin
Chelsea Stone
Cherie Heiberg
Cheryl Boudreaux
Cheyenne Smith

Chicas Poderosas
China Marsh
Chira
Chitaroni
Chris Bird, Space Hero
Chris Bong
Chris G
Chris Hourmouzis
Chris Janes
Chris Johnson
Chrissy Aitchison
Christa Seeley
Christina Bailey
Christina D'Agnillo
Christina Daniels
Christina Greengrass
Christina Haimes
Christina Hartikainen
Christine Bonadonna
Christine Jensen
Christine Miguel
Christine Moreau
Christopher D.
    Sandford
Christopher Pritchard
Chubling
Cindy Nakano
Claire & Dani
Claire & Tom Burrito
Claire & Emma Reid
Claire Chamley
Claire E. Gill
Claire Murray
Claire Pitman
Claire S.
Clare Kennedy
Classic Comics Press
Clémence Mousset
Cliff St-Onge
Clio
CMCastillo
Cockroach zine
Colin Faucett
Colin Ferguson
Colleen Gaspirc
Colleen Hillerup
Comic Nurse
Cori H
Corinne Woods
Corrina McGill
Cory Silverberg
Courtney Bates-Hardy
Craig Welsh
Cranky Aunty Lou
CrimSoul
Crystal M Rollins
Crystal Nanavati
Crystal Steltenpohl
Cynthia Huckle
Cynthia Mund
D Franklin
D. Goldstein
D. McOwen
Dallan Baumgarten
Dan Eyer
Dan Garatea
Dana Elliott
Dana Grimaldi
Danamarie Donatelli
Daniel de Segovia

Gross
Daniel Lin
Danielle & Adam
  Carey-Mooney
Danielle Bates
Danielle Bell
Danielle Calderon
Danielle Clay
Danielle Duarte
Danielle LaVaque-
  Manty
Danny Willocks
Dante
Danya Schimdt
Darian Lindle
Darren Torpey
Darryl Warcup
Dave "FD" Moraski II
Dave Wolfe
David
David A. Price
David Babbitt
David Barlex
David Bragdon
David Brook
David Byron Hudson
David Calcano
David Kruschke
David Makin
David Mariotte
David Misener
David Skoglund
David Turner
Davin Pavlas
DC & JL for our
  Russell-sprout
Dean Calkins
Deanna Halls
Debbie Cravey
Debi May
Deborah Tydings
Debra Lovelace
Deena E. Jacobs
Deft Gurl
Deirdre Aeryn
  Eisenhammer
Denis Leining
Denise Pirko
Dennis Burger
derf
Derwin Mak
Dessa Lightfoot
Desti
Destiny Torres
Di Fischer
Diamond
Diana Forster
Diana Capellan
Diane W.
DMC3004
Dominica Malcolm
Dommi Brooks
Don Alsafi
Donald E. Claxon
Donna N. Blitzen
Donyae
dorian
dorkabella
Doug Atkinson
Douglas C. LaTourette
Dr Izzi Mear
Dr. Ashley H. Hardin
Dr. Faith G. Harper
Dragon's Lair Comics
Drew Thompson
Druin
Duane Sibilly
DVB
E. Lewy
E. Panzenboeck
E.G.Hawkins
Eamonn O'Neill
EdEN
Edgy Page
Edmund Chu

Edward Chik
Eileen Gorczynski
Eileen Urban
Eileene Coscolluela
Eira A. Ekre
EldanaÂ˜ Melain
Eleanor Blair
Elissa Leach
Elizabeth Breen
Elizabeth Kenny
Elizabeth Ku
Elizabeth Newman
Elizabeth Sorrell
Elizabeth Stong
Ella Marie Peterson
Ella Quinn Lagerquist
Ellen Mellor
Emilia Hald
Emilie Montagnet
Emily Payton
Emily Crovella
Emily Davidson
Emily Hamm
Emily Leathers
Emily Miller
Emily Nelson
Emily Nisbet
Emily Norry
Emily Painter
Emily PM Johnston
Emma Draper
Emma Nix
Emmalyn & Gavin King
Emmett Elling
Endre Enyedy
entertainscape
Eric Houstoun
Eric Scott Seybert
Erick Torres
Erik T Johnson
Erika
Erin Congden
Erin Diane
Erin F.
Erin James
Erin McIntyre
Erin Millar
Erin Sayers
Erin Sullivan
Erinn Triplett
Esme Hood
Espen Selvig
Essie Bee
Esti P.
Euds Lightyear
Eunice Bae
Evan Annett
Evan H.
Evan Munday
Evan Ritchie
Evan Schmalz
Eve Golden Woods
Evelyn C
Evie Convent
Eylem Ozaslan
Faith Green
Fanie Gregoire
fantasyprone
farsaem
Fernando Del Bosque
Ferret
Flinders Jacobson
Fonzie Pants
Kaitlynne Grundner
For Sarah
Frank C.
Franklin Crosby
Fred W. Johnson
Frederick Ostrander
Freiya
Freya Benson
Future Pastimes
G. Brett Williams
GaÂ«tan Voyer-
  Perrault

Gabby Hallier
Gabriel Schlesinger
Gabriela Hernandez
  Merino
Gabriela Rodriguez
  Berón
Gabriella Tutino
Gadassik-Roginska
Gail Arlene de Vos
Gareth Bracchi
Gareth Thomas
Garreth Allen
Garrett Meek
Gary Chapple
Gary Gaines
Gary Kupczak
Gary Phillips
Gary Whitta
Gavan & Brie
Gavin "halkeye" Mogan
Gayle & Tony
Geekgirly
Gene Ha
Genevieve Tocci
Geoffrey Voss
Gianna Caiola
Gibson Grand
Gideon McKee
Gigi Griffith
Gillian McBride
Girls rock
Girls With Issues
  Podcast
GirlTuesday
Gisèle Lagacé
Glen E. Ivey
Glinelen
Golddess
Grace Waring
Graham Whiting
Grandma
Greg Elliott
Greg Lincoln
Greg McCambley
Greg Pak
GregM
guardian__J & Ursa
  Orchid
Guilded Age
Gumarx
Gwendolyn Limbach
Gwynn Grandy
H Gourley
H Haakstad
H. Anne Stoj
Hailey Conner
Haley Smith
Halina Heron
Hamish Drummond
Hamutal Argaman
Hanna Paquette
Hannah McCleary
Hannah McWhorter
Hannah Monck
Hannah Rolls
Hannah Rothman
Hannah S
Hannah Schofield
Hannah Taylor
Hannah Tsim
Happy Harbor Comics
Harky
Hassan Alamdari
Haydn Woodward
Heath Anderson
Heather B Walz
Heather Butler
Heather Farmer
Heather Fischer
Heather Martin-
  Murdoch
Heather McCann
Heather Schulte
Heidi Winkler
Helen & Skye

Helen Coates
Helen Horstmann-
  Allen
Helene Gande Drejer
Herman Duyker
Hilary B. Parton
Hilary Lawlor
Holly Aitchison
Holly Scudero
Howard Fein
Howard Hill
Hoyt Day
HR Jackson
Humanavatar
Ian Cox
Ida-Sofia
Ienilny
Ilja Preuß
Imani J Dean
IndieRed
Irene Carolyn Shaw
Irene Owen
Irene Ziemba
Ironwings
Isaac Cates
Isaac Dansicker
Isabella Blaine-Longo
Isabelle Melancon
Ivy Hang
J Á Pickford
J. C. Kassel
J. Cowley
J. Griffin Graham
J. Ross
J.M. Fenner
Jacinthe S.
Jack Baur
Jackie Dy
Jackie Miller
Jackie Spears
Jackie Stotlar
Jacob Johnson
Jacqueline Risley
Jacqueline Rothstein
Jacqui Fraser
Jade Wilson
Jade's Fire
Jaime Garmendia III
Jaime Young
Jaimie Noy
Jake Zirkle
James & Anna LeRoux
James Cooper
James H. Sullivant III
James Hampton, Jr
James Jackson
James Venhaus
James Yoho
Jamie Fong
Jamie L
Jamie Q. Pierson
Jamie Wallace
Jan Miller
Jane Edmundson
Jane Northcutt
Jane Waldner
Janelle Revord
Janelle Utheim
Janet Hetherington
Janise Deming
Janna Hochberg
Jasmine Zhou
Jason
Jason Borden
Jason E. Hall
Jason Megatron
  Burrows
Jason Murrell
Jason Price
Jason Wood
Jasper "Sharkdog"
  Barreveld
Jay Faerber
Jayme Pangalangan
JB Knibbs

JC Edualino
Jean Marsh
Jeannie Hisson
Jeff & Jess
Jeffery Sams
Jelly Bean
Jemma Neary-Grant
Jen & Éric Desmarais
Jen Costa
Jen Goertzen
Jen Leggett
Jen Stout
Jen the librarian
Jenn Duncan
Jenn Kerr
Jenn Walker
Jenna A
Jenna McPadden
Jenna Varden
Jennie Apps
Jennie Ramstad
Jennifer Annis
Jennifer Bowes
Jennifer Cross
Jennifer DePrey
Jennifer Hall
Jennifer Jenkins
Jennifer Lavoie
Jennifer McLaren
Jennifer Murphy
Jennifer Ryan
Jennifer Simonovich
Jenny Schinke
Jeremy Ladan
Jeroen vd Gulik
Jess Paine
Jess Scott
Jessamy
Jesse McGatha
Jesse Richards
Jessi & Davis
Jessi Jordan
Jessica "busdjur"
  Rickardsson
Jessica Abel
Jessica Berglund
Jessica Enfante
Jessica Heselschwerdt
Jessica Milagros Chew
  Baca Delgadillo
Jessica mills
Jessica Paoli
Jessica Powell
Jessica Silverstein
Jessie Barr
Jessie G.
Jessy Beaulieu
Jez Horbury
Jill Jamieson
Jill Valuet
Jim Bradfield
Jim Scheel
Jim Wood
Jimmy Law
JLee
JM Wong
Jo Hacker
Joana Almeida & India
  Morris
Jody Broad
Joe Fusion
Joe Toole
Joe Watkins
Joel Chahal
John Alfred Young
John Bretana
John Brownlee
John C Barstow
John Carr (Mezada)
John D. Roberts
John Henry
John Kyritsis
John Newquist
John Paizs
John Potten

John Tinkess
John Wimmer
Jon Pinyan
Jonathan Barnett
Jonathan Burroughs
Jonathan Chiaravalle
Jonathan Edwards
Jonathan Irvine
Joonw93
JoPM
Jose Alfredo Villalobos
Joseph Zelada
Josh Muller
Josh Crews Night Nurse
Josh Maher
Josh Rain
Josh Shapel
Josh Wilson
Joshua Hilderbrand
Joshua James Gervais
Joshua Matchett
Joshua Munro
Josie Vimahi
Joslyn Dechant
Judith Collard
Jules K. Walker
Jules Philippe Laurent
 de Bellefeuille Defoy
Julian Wharton
Julie Grant
Julie Hayes
Julie McGee
Julie Young
Jun Jie
June Jenssen
June Shieh
Justin Snyder
Justus
JW
K. M. Cooper
K. Rodenberger
K.Morgan-May
Kadie Yale
Kadri
Kae Richardson
Kaela Feit
Kaitlyn Till
Kalaya W.
Karen Devotta
Karen DeWysockie
Karen Green
Karen McDonough
Karen Peper/Sue
 Gerrity
Karen Roberts
Kari Little
Kari Maaren
Karin & Patrick
 Weekes
Karine Charlebois
Karthik Kakarala
Kassie Kay Avant
Kat
Kat Denvir
Kat Kennewell
Kat Nakaji
Kat Newman
Kate Andrews Hoult
Kate Baker
Kate Clifford
Kate Hillier
Kate Laird
Kate Land & Chris
 Hutten-Czapski
Kate Malloy
Kate R
Kate Richards
Kateisgreat
katha
Katherine Hanson
Katherine Hempel
Katherine Mereand-
 Sinha
Katherine S
Katherine Stratton

Kathleen & Max
Kathleen Erickson
Kathryn Awesome
Kathryn B
Kathryn Cummins
Kathryn Gudsnuk
Katie Büttner
Katie Boudreaux
Katie Dungar
Katie Eberle
Katie Elliott
Katie Foster
Katie Goodrich
Katie Ledford
Katie McDowell
Katie Peters
Katie Sullivan
Katie Swanson
Katrina Rittershofer
Katy Rex
Kaylee Thomas
Kazgrinega
Keegan King
Keidy Zuniga
Keight MacLean
Keiji Miashin
Keiren Smith/Ty
 Templeton
Keith Frady
Keith Maillard
Kelly & Marjorie Walsh
Kelly Breswick
Kelly Chettle
Kelly Fitzpatrick
Kelly Hoolihan
Kelly Moravec
Kelly Ziemski
Kellyn Hoffman
Kelsey M Avril
Kelsey Thomson
Kelsey Wozniak
Ken Steacy
Kent Akselsen
Keroan
Kerry Smith
Kevin Fitzgerald
Kevin J. "Womzilla"
 Maroney
Kevin Meville
KFaber
Kicklix
Kim & Kathleen
 Williams
Kim MacDonald
Kim Pittman
Kim Tompkins
kimberly ann
Kimberly H.
Kinari Horton
Kingston Gaming
 Nexus
Kira Jones
Kira Mandel
Kirsten Korona
Kirsty Win
Kishmatic
Kitfox
Komala Singh
Kris Phelps
KrishaSong Parkey
 Miller
Krista Majewski
Kristen C.
Kristen Gentile
Kristen Madrid
Kristen Northrup
Kristian Bruun
Kristin W.
Kristoffer Saylor
Kristy Quinn
Krystal Tubbs
Ksenia Winnicki
Kyla Blythe-Prahl
Kylie Wells
kyoki

Lacey Marshall
Lara Mathews
Larissa Haluszka-
 Smith
Larissa Lay
Larsson Youngberg
Laura & Michael
 Spiegel
Laura Bastlover
Laura Berestecki
Laura Brenner
Laura C. Morales
Laura Christiansen
Laura Drew
Laura Gluhanich
Laura Indick
Laura Lawson
Laura Markham
Laura Seul Gallagher
Laura Simpson
Laura White
Lauracet McIntyre
Lauren Chochinov
Lauren Dombrowski
Lauren E. Bradley
Lauren Isaacson
Lauren M. McClain
Lauren Parker
Lauren Scanlan
Lauren Winslow
 Salinas
Laurent Lehmann
Laurie A. MacDougall
Leah Spano
Leen Isabel
Leigh Buholtz
Leigh Challoner
Leigh Ward-Broussard
Lel
Lene Andersen
Lennhoff Family
Leonard Hoffman
Leonard Stanwick
Leslie Doyle
Leslie Larkins
Leslie Lyles
Lethargic Studios
Levi Fleming
Lewis
Liam Conlon
Liam E
Liam Stewart
Lianne
Lilian Min
Liliana Ritzmann
Lily Roth
Lily Zamanali
Lindsey Bieda
Linnea Samila
Lisa Heermann
Lisa Heinen
Lisa M
Lisa Rabey
Lisa Thomson
Lisa Visser
Liz Bruton
Liz Coleman
Liz Colombo
Liz G.
Liz Huang
Liz Schiller
Liz Van Pelt
Lizzette Walls
Lizzie Roper
Lizzy Allman
LJ Maher
locallyunscene
Lorena Landeros
Lori Brown
Lori hymowitz
Lorimuni
Loving Geek Girl!
Lucinda May Edwards
Lucy Kelsall
lustigit

Lux
Lynne
M Chowning
M. Howalt
M. Trembath
Macy Lao
Maddy Beaupre
Madison Cawker
Maeve Adams
Maggie McLean
Maggie Shanks
Maggie Waldmyer
Mainon A. Schwartz
Maithê Rosa
Maitland Lederer
Mallory Duriak
Malory Lyness
Manoshi Quayes
Marenka
Margaret Kroehler
Margaret St.John
Maria A. Phillis
Maria Norris
Maria Sandmo
Maria Shirey
Maria Young
Mariana Sosa
mariaqqch
Marie Bannister
Marie K.
marie mour
Marie-Anne D.
Marikka Hughes
Marion Waltamath
Maris Kreizman
Marit Freya
Marjorie Mordido
Mark Eliot
Mark Mikulec
Mark Schutt
Mark Strange
Mark T. Byzewski
MarlysPop
Mary K Gottschalk
Mary Spielman
Mary Van Tyne
Marybeth Yarosh
Mathilde Tamae-
 Bouhon
Matt Chin
Matt Fox
Matt Larson
Matt Morin
Matt Payte
Matt Zweig
Matthew Haycock
Matthew Oliphant
Mawusime Blewuada
Max Anderson
Max Hawkins
Max Shannon
Max Zomborszki
Maya Fox
Maya Woods
Meg Fisher
Meg Osborn
Meg Smitherman
Meg W.
Megan Brown
Megan Byrd
Megan D.
Megan Heggs
Megan L-L
Megan Mackay
Megan Mania
Meghan Blythe Adams
Meghan Malone
Meghan McNeight
Meghan Normandin
Meghan Potts
Mel
Mel Huston Taylor
Mel Thomas
Mel Trender
Melanie Baker

Melanie Rebekah
Melinda Hawes
Melinda V. Stanley
Melissa Dalgleish
Melissa Mae
Melissa Markle
Melissa Whitlock
Merak Z
Mhairi Summers
Mia Cameron
 McDonald
Mia Moore
mic fok
Michael Carens-
 Nedelsky
Michael David
Michael Ederer
Michael Kwan
Michael Satran
Michael Steamweed
Michaela Dalbert
Michele
Michele Haggar
Michele McPherson
Michelle Cooper
Michelle Cristiani
Michelle Everhart
Michelle Humphries
Michelle Johnson
Michelle Palmer
Michelle Quirk
Michelle Villanueva
Michelle Y. Morris
Mickey Spencer
Mike Aragona
Mike Cassella
Mike Pellerito
Mikkel Thomas
Min Nemoy
Miranda Harmon
Miranda Hutchinson
Miranda Thomas-
 Sailors
Miriam Cohen Kiel
Miriam Oudin
Mo Reyes
MoLith
Mollee Marcus
Mollie Flanagan
Molly Brewer
Molly Cady
Molly D. Elliott
Molly J. Scanlon
Molly Miller
Molly Stewart-Cohn
Monica Baker
Monica Heitman
Monica Marlowe
Moonfern
Moose Rogers
Morgan Winer
Moshe Prigan
Mother of Constraints
My Lemon
MyKDE
Myles Braithwaite
N. C. Christopher
 Couch, Ph.D.
Nadav Lifschits
Nalin Lindqvist
Name listed
Nancy Bray
Nancy Calvert-Warren
Nancy Do
Nancy Joyce
Nancy Spindler
Naomi Hyndman
Naomi I. Johnson
Naomi Mercer
Naomi Rath
Nasreen Bandali
Natalie Coish
Natalie Proracki
Nathan Schulz
Nathaniel

Neil Graham
neko4
Nelson Pecora
Nia Bock
Nicholas J. McBurney
Nicholas Vanderburg
Nick Furze
Nick Goodway
Nick Guerrera
Nick 'Hijump' Russ
Nick Lapeyrouse
Nico D.
Nicola Pravato
Nicolas Longtin-Martel
Nicole Adelle Rich
Nicole Eschen Solis
Nicole Glade
Nicole Knight
Nicole Mortenson
Nicole Sobon
Nigel Allen
Nigel Roberts
Nigel Tangelo
Nikki Jeske
Nikki Zano
Nina Raoof
Nivea
Noam
Noam Weiss
Ola Boström
Olivia
Olivia Jacocks
Oni Press
Orastes
Oriana A Hills
Osakioduwa
Ottawa Writers Festival
ottero
P Aiken
P Noguchi
Page Birmingham
Paige Luther
Paisley Conrad
Paola Paulino
Paris
Patricia Sanvictores
Pattie Miller
Patty King
Paul C Robinson
Paul Calhoun
Paul Freelend
Paul Paterson
Paul R Benson
Paul S. Dwyer
Pete hamboussi
Peter Henderson
Phil Hester
Philip Saaltink
Phylicia P.
Pierce B.
PistachioRoux
Pixie Walker
PL
PL Hunt
princeodd
Prox & Firs
Psuedonomymous
psy
Pulp Literature Press
Quinn Stephens
R. E. Hammond
R. Louis Carreiro
R. Robineau
R.J.H.
Rabia Sitabi (RPISH)
Rachael Collins & Matt
    Schneider
Rachael Haggerty
Rachael Swiss
Rachél Bazelais
Rachel D.
Rachel Davies
Rachel Eaton

Rachel Maeroff
Rachel Willis
Rachelle Abellar
Rain & Aidenn
Randall Kirby
Randi Misterka
Ravensdance
Ray Powell
Rebecca Beard
Rebecca Duddington
Rebecca Epstein
Rebecca Fay Hoffman
Rebecca Greetis
Rebecca Grieser
Rebecca Kuglitsch
Rebecca Rahrer
Rebecca T.
Rebecca Wilcox
Regis M. Donovan
remur
Renaud Bédard
Renée S Krulich
Rhian Standley
Rhiannon Burner
Rhiannon Raphael
Richard & Amber
    Davis
Ridley Kemp
Rik & Sabrina
    Spruitenburg
Riley Le Cocq
Risë Taylor
Rob & Libby
Rob Atwood
Rob Millman
Rob Zeroun
Robber Tom
robert duckworth
Robert Gilson
Robert M. Chute
Robert Usarek
Roberta Abrams
Robin C.
Robin Swindell
Rodney Carter
rodney elin
Rodrigo Ortiz Vinholo
Roger B.A. Klorese &
    David Haney
Roland Glasser
Rolando A. Alvarez Jr.
Ron & Sara Carroll
Rosalia
Rosanna Lam
Rosanna Viirre & Erik
    Viirre
Rose DiLoreto
Rose Mocerino
Roslyn Davidson
Rowan, Darsey &
    Cailean
Rowena Knill
Rowland Gwynne
Roxanne Grondin
Rufus Orsborne
Rus Wooton
Ryan "Muscles" North
Ryan Ashe
Ryan Breedon
Ryan DiSanto
Ryan H
Ryan J Joseph
Ryan McCulloch
Ryan Oliver
Ryan Palmer
S. Zupon
S.E. Andres
S.M. Beiko
Saadia Muzaffar
Sadie Ogan
Sahana Puvirajasingam
SallyRose Robinson
Sam Keeney

Sam Le Beau
Sam Power
Sam Wachter
Samantha Cantwell
Samantha Chin
Samantha David
Samantha Elizabeth
    Schaffer
Samantha Jones
Samantha Martin
Samantha N.
Samantha Staddon
Sami
Sammy K.
Sandra R. Carbone
Sanjay Dharawat
Sanna Bo Claumarch
Sara Crow
Sara Ghaleb
Sara Hewitt
Sara Macanovic
Sara Strauss
Sarah Ann Head
Sarah Benkin
Sarah Boyle
Sarah Bricker-Carter
Sarah E. Stumpf
Sarah Frisk
Sarah Holt
Sarah King
Sarah L. Robinson
Sarah Liberman
Sarah Livingston
Sarah McMullanNZ
Sarah Scherbatsky
Sarah Scholz
Sarah Sharp
Sarah Thrasher
Sarah Uhl
Sashah Li
Savage
Scitchet
Scott Chantler
Scott Forgue
Scott K. Johnson
Scott Martin
Scott Pohlenz
Scott Rosen
Scott Schaper
Scott Susans
Scott Wenter
Sean Bonner
Sean Frost
Sean Lynch & Alexis
    Cabrerra
Sean Murphy
Sean P. Aune
Sebastian Jauert
Sebastian Simson
Sela Davis
Seraphina Ferraro
Serephita
Shan de Leers
Shane W Berry
Shanna Brockmeyer
Shanna Hollich
Shanna Mullen
Shannon
    Christoffersen
Shannon Kauderer
Shannon Moffett
Shari Huxtable
Sharon K.
Sharon Wong
Sharona Ginsberg
Shauna & Maddy E
Shawn Manley
Shean, Semeicha
    & Sapphira
    Mohammed
Sheilah Villari
Shelby Bennett
Shell Graves

Shelley K. Fassler
Shelly & David Alan
Sheri Dubuc
Shield Bonnichsen
Shiri Rokshin
Shoontz
Silvana Moro
silvermare
Skayne
Skuggi
SM
Snaking Bend Rover
    Family
Snow McNally
Solange Morales
Solitary Spinster
Sonja S
Sophia McKissick
Sophie
Sophie Forsyth
Sophie Overett
Soren Moskjaer
    Lauridsen
Sparkle Cunt
splendidgeek
spongefile
SPS
Stacey Linda Boden
Stefan Kaszycki
Stefanie Ryan
stellans
Steph Pouliotte
Stephanie Fisher
Stephanie Mallory
Stephanie N Noell
Stephanie Rosario
Stephanie Russo
Stephanie Shena
Stephanie Wong
Stephen E Kacir
Stephen Patrick
Steve Hendricks
Steve M. Fletcher
Steve Siri
Steven Lu
Steven R. Staton
Strange Adventures
Stu Trent
Sue Ann Barber
Sunfell
SupaCindy3000
Surka Sapphire
Susan L.
Susan McCarthy
Susan McCurdy
Susannah Gast
Suzanne Wallace
Suzette Padley
Swapna Krishna
Sweta M.
Sylvia Vathis
T. E. Davidson
T. Holmes
T.A. Pujol
T.X. Watson
Tabby Rose
Tacwolf
Takeshi Takahashi
Tamara C. Larsen
Tamara Murray
Tamara Ricarda
Tamea McIntosh
Tamera Burnett
Tammy Lee
Tammy Meyer
Tammy Sunwall
Tara & Neil Scott
Tara K. Reed
Taylor Hoffman
Taylor LaBresh
Taylor von Kugelgen
Team Denson
Ten Van Winkle

Teresa J Wood
Teri Trewolla
Tess Sutton
The Beguiling Books
the fire starter
The Green Machine
The Nani-Lama
The Tot.
TheGeek
theoreticallye
theredphone
Theresa N. Rojas
Thiago Fontes
Thijs
Thomas Polok
Thomas Willoughby
Tiff Hudson
Tiffany Kuang
Tiffany To
Tim Meakins
Tim Mottishaw
timlmul
Tina-Marie A. Venus
Tony Montuori
Tony Yeh
Traci Hlafka
Traci Olsen
Travis Teitsch
Treve Hodsman
Trevor Boytinck
Tricia Rosetty
Trillian Tyler
Trina Blake
Tris Harding
Trista Bishop-Watt
Truthiness
TSine
Tuuli S
Tyler Overby
Val Freire
Valerie & Aaron Cahan
Valerie E. Polichar
Veronica I. Arreola
Viannah E. Duncan
Vicki Hsu
Vicki Lantz
Vicky Bugg
Victor Campa
Vincent & Salem
    Dacak
Vinod Viswanath
Violette Hutchins
Virginia Van Diest
voodooengineer
    @gmail.com
vravenus
VsquaredK
Wally Hastings
Wendy Zita
WhiskeyRae
Will Chernoff
Will Ludwigsen
William Anderson
Willow A. Flint
Woon Yong Xin
    Chrysalis
Yorick Phoenix &
    Karen Williams
YoriKv
Zachary Caton
Zak Bryson
Zee
Zee Thornton
Zesty-Chef
Ziva & zorro
Zoe Hayes
Zoë Steel
Zoe Walker
Zosha Sugarbear